Birthing Your
DREAMS

GOD'S PLAN FOR LIVING VICTORIOUSLY

THOMAS NELSON PUBLISHERS®

Nashville

Birthing Your
DREAMS

GOD'S PLAN FOR LIVING VICTORIOUSLY

PAULA WHITE

THOMAS NELSON PUBLISHERS®
Nashville

Published by Thomas Nelson, Inc.
P.O. Box 141000
Nashville, TN 37214

Scripture taken from The Holy Bible, New King James Version (NKJV). Copyright 1979, 1980, 1982 by Thomas Nelson, Inc. Used by permission. All rights reserved.

Library of Congress Cataloging-in-Publication Data is available.

ISBN: 0-7852-5069-7

Printed in United States of America

03 04 05 06 07 – 5 4 3 2 1

Foreword

Dreams. We all have them. But in the realm of hopes and dreams are two kinds of people: the "haves" and the "have-nots." Some people never move beyond the exercise of dreaming to see their dreams come true. Likewise, everyone has a destiny, but not everyone reaches it.

I want you to walk in the fullness of your destiny and to see all your dreams come true! But I know that you have a part to play in their fulfillment. I know that you must bring your dreams to birth—and I believe you can do it!

This workbook will help you bring to birth all the promises and potential that are stirring inside of you, and I know of no one more qualified to call forth the destiny of God in you than the gifted, anointed, dynamic preacher, and teacher— Pastor Paula White. You may know her for her challenging Bible teaching, or by way of her extensive television ministry, or as co-pastor of the thriving Without Walls International Church in Tampa, Florida. But for now, allow her to be your labor coach as you bring your dreams to birth. Let her motivate you, within these pages, to be all you are called and created to be as one of God's leading ladies!

In order to help you get started, I'd like to take a moment to walk you through each of the features you will find in the pages of this workbook so that you will understand why we have included them and what I hope your interaction with them will accomplish in your life.

Introducing . . .: The word speaks for itself. Introductions to each chapter will simply show you the big picture of the subject covered and give you a glimpse of where we are headed in that chapter.

The Main Event: I am delighted by the wealth of sound, practical advice and godly wisdom in this workbook. This helpful information is presented to you in sections entitled, "The Main Event," which is divided into "Acts," just as a stage play is divided into acts. Each act focuses specifically on a particular aspect of the larger subject of the chapter.

You're On: One of my hopes for you as you work through this book is that you will find all kinds of ways to apply its information to its own life. To help you in that purpose, we have included some questions for you to answer. I hope you'll think about them, answer them, and even use an extra sheet of paper or your journal if you find yourself wanting to consider them more thoroughly or respond to them more extensively.

Learn Your Lines: You probably know that God's Word is "living and active," as we read in the Book of Hebrews, but I want you to continue to experience its transforming power in your daily life. Therefore at the end of many acts, you will find several scriptures relating to the subject you have just studied. As the Word gets worked into your mind, it gets worked out in your life, so I believe these scriptures really are keys to help you unlock personal victory and success.

Coming Soon: I love this part of the workbook because it is your opportunity to dream on paper. These beautifully designed pages at the end of each chapter will allow you to write a synopsis of what you have learned throughout that chapter, to summarize how you will put those lessons into practice and to take time to really think about your life and your hopes, aspirations, and inspirations into written form.

Action!: Goal-setting is so important to successful living, and that is why we have concluded every chapter with space for you to list specific goals pertaining to the topic of that chapter. I encourage you to use that space to set a few measurable, challenging, attainable goals and to give yourself a deadline and a reward for reaching each one. In the back of the workbook you will find an Appendix in which you can put all your goals together on one list and prioritize them.

Leading Lady, the lights are coming up, and it is time for you to live the dreams that have been backstage, in the depths of your heart for so long. I hope you will enjoy this workbook and that it will help you identify and embrace God's dreams for your life and give you the courage to go after them with all of your heart.

God bless you,
T. D. Jakes

Contents

Introduction

Because I know you are a leading lady, I believe that God has put a dream in your heart. And your dream is your destiny! You may just now be discovering God's dream for your life, or you may have been carrying it for years. Whatever the case, I am here to help you see that dream come true.

Before we get started, I want to make sure you know that God is not offended by your aspirations. He is not intimidated by your pursuit. In fact, God is the One who put those dreams and desires in you in the first place—and He wants to bring them to pass. Psalm 21:1 says, "You have given him his heart's desire, and have not withheld the request of his lips."

Perhaps you have heard of Nelson Mandela, who spent 27 years in prison before becoming president of South Africa. He said something that I want you to read and understand: "Your playing small does not serve this world." Do you see that? "Your playing small does not serve this world." What does it mean? In "leading lady language," it means that, if you are going to take your place on center stage and make a difference in this world, you are going to put one foot in front of the other and walk into the spotlight. You are going to have to do some things in order to bring your dreams to birth. In this workbook, I'm going to help you identify what you need to do and how you need to do it.

When desire penetrates potential, it conceives reality. I believe now is the time for that to happen in your life. It is time for your potential as one of God's leading ladies to invade the desires He has put in your heart and for His purposes to burst into full bloom.

Leading lady, I stir up the gift of God that is within you right now. I have faith for all His purposes to come to pass in your life. I'm here to pull the greatness out of you and call you to largeness. I speak to you the words of Isaiah 60:1, "Arise, shine; for your light has come! And the glory of the Lord is risen upon you." I call you to come forth! I call for the destiny within you to emerge! And I call those dreams to come to birth!

1

The Lady
Dares to Dream

Introducing

ne of the greatest gifts you have in your life is the ability to see beyond your present state—to dream. As long as you are alive, there is a dream within you. You may not label it as such, but I assure you there is a dream within you—and it is all about God's great purposes and plans for your life and the lives you will touch as you fulfill the destiny He has designed for you. No one can define your dream but you. God gives your dream to you alone, and it is your job to be a good steward of the vision and the passion with which He has entrusted you. I would go so far as to say that it is not up to God to create a destiny for you; it is up to you to discover the destiny that has already been created for you. The dream is within you; all you have to do is choose to embrace it. Are you ready? Here we go.

The Main Event

Act 1: I Dare You

I'm sure you've heard it said that God never asks us to handle more than we can bear, but when it comes to the dreams He puts in our hearts, there is always a certain amount of challenge when it comes to seeing them fulfilled. God does not change His mind once He calls a leading lady or places an assignment on her life, but He does not make the fulfillment of that assignment easy or a "no brainer." He does, however, make it well worth the effort it will take to see the dream come to pass. Just think about it: if you were a runner, you would treasure a first-place medal for a marathon more than a first place medal for running 10 yards. Why? Because the victory would have cost you so much more. Lots of people can run 10 yards, but a marathon victory requires training and practice and dedication. In the end, though, the satisfaction of winning (or even completing the course!) is deep and rich.

So it is with your dream. It will stretch you. It will challenge you, inspire, you and frustrate you. I dare you to hold fast to that burning desire in your heart, that longing, that unction down deep inside of you, that call you can hear above the loudest noise. It keeps you awake at night; it captures your attention by day and you are unable to shake it. When

> *Your dream will stretch you. It will challenge you, inspire you, and frustrate you. I dare you to hold fast to that burning desire in your heart, that longing, that unction down deep inside of you, that call you can hear above the loudest noise.*

God puts a dream in your heart, as I know He has, it gives you the desire and momentum to pursue your goal, and it dispenses an unquenchable desire to accomplish things you have never done.

When God plants a dream in a chosen vessel (that's you!), it's not because He needs you to accomplish that thing; rather, God is allowing you to participate in His accomplishments. There are many undis-covered, unused or under-utilized gifts, talents and abilities lying dormant within you waiting to be activated by your willingness to birth the dream inside of you. I believe God is calling you from your destined state and not our present state. He has the ability to see you as you are going to become. Since He believes in you and sees all you can be, isn't it time for you to believe in yourself and dream the dreams of a lifetime? I just dare you to discover God's dream for your life and bring it forth. Yes, I dare you. I double-dog dare you to dream!

One of the greatest gifts you have in your life is the ability to see beyond your present state — to dream.

You're On

1. What do you believe your God-given dreams are? Note them briefly below.

_____

_____

_____

_____

_____

_____

2. Rate yourself. On a scale of 1-10, with 10 being terrific and 1 being lousy, how have you handled or stewarded your dream. (Now be honest. If you aren't doing a good job, then this workbook will teach you how!)

_____

_____

_____

_____

> *"Your playing small does not serve this world."*
> Nelson Mandela

3. Now for the moment of truth. I dare you to dream. What do you say?

_____

_____

_____

_____

Learn Your Lines

For I know the thoughts that I think toward you,
says the Lord, thoughts of peace and not of evil,
to give you a future and a hope.
Jeremiah 29:11

Do you not know that those who run in a
race all run, but one receives the prize?
Run in such a way that you may obtain it.
1 Corinthians 9:24

I can do all things through Christ who strengthens me.
Philippians 4:13

Act 2: What's the Big Deal?

You may be wondering why I would dare you to dream, why I would not just gently encourage you or make a mere suggestion that you might want to consider dreaming a dream. Why do you think I find it necessary to dare you? I'll tell you—because I know that to dream is to commit yourself to a daring adventure. To dream is to stretch, to risk, to stay confident in the face of uncertainty, and to be willing to encounter and overcome opposition. I have devoted an entire chapter in this book to waging spiritual war over your dreams and to strategies for victory, but for now, you simply need to be aware that your dream is a target for the enemy.

Yes, the enemy is out to kill your dreams. He is not after you so much as he is after your destiny, your dreams. He knows that you will deal a lethal blow to his dark kingdom if you are allowed to reach your full potential in God and to fulfill God's plans for your life—so he is actively and continually plotting the downfall of your destiny and scheming to destroy the dreams within you.

> *To dream is to commit yourself to a daring adventure. To dream is to stretch, to risk, to stay confident in the face of uncertainty, and to be willing to encounter and overcome opposition*

Graveyards are filled with poems that were never written, songs that were never sung, sermons that were never preached, books that were never published, and businesses that were never birthed. All of those things were once dreams in someone's heart, but for some reason, the enemy was able to keep them from being fulfilled. But I need to tell you that this is nothing new! The devil has been trying to kill dreams and dreamers for thousands of years. Look at what happened to Joseph:

> *Now when they saw him afar off, even before he came near them, they conspired against him to kill him. Then they said to one another, "Look, this dreamer is coming! Come therefore, let us now kill him and cast him into some pit; and we shall say, 'Some wild beast has devoured him.' We shall see what will become of his dreams!" (Gen. 37:18-20).*

If you are serious about seeing your dreams come true, you will have to wrestle with the question: *What will become of your dreams?* I would be remiss to not tell you that they will most likely die at the enemy's hand if you do not guard them, nourish them, and do everything within your power, with God's help, to bring them to pass. You are more than a conqueror in Christ, and in Him, your victory is secure—

but won't come without a fight! The dream, you see, has much greater potential than the dreamer. Knowing you will win because of Jesus, are you ready to take to the battle?

You're On

1. Can you think of specific times when you knew the enemy was trying to kill the dreams inside of you? List them here.

_____

_____

_____

_____

_____

2. Is there anything going on in your life right now that seems to be an attempt by the enemy to kill your dream or de-rail your destiny?

_____

_____

_____

_____

_____

If you are serious about seeing your dreams come true, you will have to wrestle with the question: What will become of your dreams?

3. How can you proactively combat and stand against the enemy's efforts to steal, kill or destroy your God-given dream?

_____

_____

_____

_____

_____

_____

_____

4. Are you willing to take the dare and to fight for the dream God has placed in your heart?

_____

_____

_____

_____

_____

_____

_____

5. Would you make a faith statement right now by answering this question: What will become of your dreams?

_____

_____

_____

_____

_____

_____

Learn Your Lines

The thief does not come except to kill, and to kill, and to destroy.
I have come that they may have life, and that they may have it more abundantly.
John 10:10

. . .lest Satan take advantage of us; for we are not ignorant of his devices.
2 Corinthians 2:11

For we do not wrestle against flesh and blood, but against principalities, against powers, against the rulers of the darkness of this age, against spiritual hosts of wickedness in the heavenly places.
Ephesians 6:12

COMING SOON

As you think about taking the dare to dream, take a few moments to jot down your dreams. You may have written them in question 1 of Act 1, but now is the time to expand and write down everything that comes to mind as you think about your dreams. How are you going to steward that which God has placed in your heart? What will life look like for you as you win the war over your dreams? What changes do you need to make in your life in order to accommodate your dreams? What great things do you long for and believe will happen as you pursue your dream?

_____

_____

_____

_____

_____

_____

_____

_____

_____

_____

ACTION!

*B*ased on what you have learned in this chapter, what are three concise, measurable, attainable goals you will set for yourself as you dare to dream? Be sure to include a schedule and target date for reaching each goal and a reward for accomplishing it.

1. Goal: _____

Schedule and target completion date: _____

Reward: _____

_____

2. Goal: _____

Schedule and target completion date: _____

Reward: _____

_____

3. Goal: _____

Schedule and target completion date: _____

Reward: _____

_____

2

The Lady Lets God Lead

Introducing

Leading ladies tend to be strong, confident and perfectly able to manage their busy lives and fulfill their dreams. But I really want to challenge you in this chapter to make sure that the dreams and aspirations you are pursuing are of the Lord and are not products of your own mind or of someone else's expectations or desires for you. You are a bright and capable woman, and the best way to invest your brainpower and abilities is to pour your energies into fulfilling the dreams God has for you. Now is a good time to take a look at your dreams and make sure your dreams are His dreams for your life. If you need to make some adjustments, I'll help you know how to begin to identify just what His plans and purposes are. Let's think through these matters together for a few moments right now, as you let God lead you into His exciting, fulfilling dreams for your life.

The Main Event

Act 1: Dividing Soul and Spirit

Women seem to be born with the capacity to dream. Unfortunately, our society, at least in America, has preyed upon this God-given tendency and attempted to lure us into the dangerous realm of fantasy. Do you know what I mean? As little girls, we hear fairy tales of princes and princesses and read the stories of damsels in distress and knights in shining armor. As young women, we watch television shows that can cause us to drool over handsome men and want to imitate beautiful women. As adults, we could fill every weekday afternoon with soap operas and the rest of our time with romance novels! And what do these things do to us if we are not careful? They can cause us to fantasize about lives that are not real and perhaps, even about imaginary lovers. They can allow us to escape reality in favor of something more glamorous. They can set false expectations of lives we would like to live.

> *Women seem to be born with the capacity to dream.*

I need to tell you that leading ladies lead real lives. We do not take part in fantasy of any sort. We do not let a television show or a romance novel cause us to long for the kind of life that only exists on a screen—even if the screen is just in our own minds. We do not admire or lust after fictional characters, and we do not take lessons from make-believe people.

Why am I being so strong about this issue of women and fantasy? Because I know how dangerous it can be. I have seen so many women miss their own lives because they live in a fantasy world. And we don't encounter God in fantasy;

we encounter God in real life. He deals with us in nitty-gritty, everyday, ordinary reality. It is crucial that we learn to see through the eyes of the Spirit and not through our imaginations.

When I write to you about your dreams, I want to make sure that your dreams are born of the Spirit and not of the soul. "Soulish dreams" originate in your soul—your mind, will or emotions. They are the dreams you dream for yourself, and they can have their source in some kind of fantasy. On the other hand, God's dreams for you are birthed in the realm of the Spirit; they are planted in your heart by the Holy Spirit, and they are nourished by His ministry in your life.

I want to help you discover the dreams God has for you. But first, let's make sure that those old soulish dreams get cleaned out of you so that there is room enough in your heart to hold the dreams of the Lord. As we begin to separate the dreams of your soul from the dreams of God's Spirit, let me share with you a common experience among women when it comes to their own dreams. One of the areas that is often most affected by soulish dreams is the arena of love and marriage. Many women grow up with visions of "Mr. Right" or with hopes that they will marry a man with certain physical characteristics, such as "six-pack" abs or a football-player physique. Some women dream of marrying a doctor or a lawyer or a powerfully anointed minister of the gospel. Some dream of marrying a man who has achieved a specific level of education or enjoys a certain financial status. They then go on to dream of beautiful homes and "perfect" children and eventually, a comfortable retirement on the beach!

Leading ladies lead real lives.

I do believe it is possible for the Lord to give a woman a true Spirit-born vision for her marriage, but far too many women take their cues from the media or from other people and begin to imagine lovers and love stories that simply are not of God. This kind of fantasy is not exclusive to love and marriage; it can also be at work in the area of the material possessions you dream of or in terms of your career.

Before you answer the questions below, think about dreams that have been influenced by the media or by something you have observed in someone else's life. Think also about dreams that were in your heart before you became a believer or before you began seeking God earnestly about His plans for your life.

> *God's dreams for you are birthed in the realm of the Spirit; they are planted in your heart by the Holy Spirit and they are nourished by His ministry in your life.*

You're On

1. What soulish dreams have you dreamed for yourself?

_____

_____

_____

_____

_____

_____

_____

2. Can you remember a specific movie, television show or book that caused you to want the kind of life that was depicted on the screen or in print? What was it? Pray now and ask the Holy Spirit to help you remember, and then list everything that comes to your mind.

_____

_____

_____

_____

3. Have you ever wished or pretended that you were a character you saw in a movie or on television or that you read about in a book? Have you ever wished or pretended that you had a relationship with someone you watched or read about? (This is common among adolescent girls and teenagers, so look back that far in your life. "Crushes" on movie stars or athletes can move beyond the "crush" into unhealthy behavior such as lust or other fantasy.) Pray now, and ask the Holy Spirit to help you remember, and then list everything that comes to your mind.

_____

_____

_____

_____

_____

4. What has been the result of the soulish dreams you have made up for yourself? (I have a hunch they've brought much frustration!)

_____

_____

_____

_____

_____

5. Look at your answers to questions 2 and 3, bearing in mind that we ask the Holy Spirit to bring up certain issues like these so that we can repent. Then, we can be cleansed and set free to dream the dreams of God for our lives. Confess the situations in which you allowed anything that was not of God to influence your hopes for the future and your dreams for your life. Repent for each specific instance and receive His forgiveness. Release all your soulish dreams, and ask the Lord to wash their influence from you completely. He'll do it!

_____

_____

_____

_____

_____

6. Now, are you ready and willing to embrace God's dreams for your life?

_____

_____

_____

_____

_____

_____

_____

God's anointing and His favor tend to accompany His dreams for your life.

Learn Your Lines

Trust in the Lord with all your heart, and lean not on your own understanding; in all your ways acknowledge Him, and He shall direct your paths.

Proverbs 3:5, 6

If we confess our sins, He is faithful and just to forgive us our sins and to cleanse us from all unrighteousness.

1 John 1:9

For all that is in the world—the lust of the flesh, the lust of the eyes, and the pride of life—is not of the Father but is of the world.

1 John 2:16

Act 2: Discovering Your Dreams

So how do you know what your dream really is? How can you identify the dreams God has placed in your heart? Finding God's will is a continuous activity that will be a part of your life until you go to heaven, but let me suggest two activities that will help you as you seek His dreams for you: watch and pray.

When I tell you to watch, I mean for you to look inside yourself and watch to see what moves and stirs you. Watch your reactions to situations and events. Watch to see what evokes your passion, your affection, or your anger. Watch to see what you are willing to sacrifice for. Watch for the natural abilities and affinities and giftings that rise to the surface over the course of your life. Watch to see what you are interested in and what you are drawn to.

> *Finding God's will is a continuous activity that will be a part of your life until you go to heaven, but let me suggest two activities that will help you as you seek His dreams for you: watch and pray.*

For example, let's say that you become aware of an opportunity to help underprivileged children in your community. You feel compassion in your heart toward the children and something inside of you feels compelled to help. You make a phone call and discover that you can help by going to the community center and reading stories to the children on Tuesday afternoons. But, uh-oh, your favorite television show is on at the same time. You don't care; you skip the show and go read to the children. You are so fulfilled after you have finished that you forgot all about the television program you missed. Hmmm—there may be a dream inside of you, a dream to make a difference in the lives of children.

Let's think about another example. Perhaps you loved music as a little girl. Everywhere you went, there was a song in your heart and on your lips. When you were old enough, you were willing to practice the piano instead of playing outside with the other children. Even now, when you are down or frustrated, you will sing or play an instrument and the music soothes you. I think there might be a dream inside of you—to be a worship leader, a music teacher, a member of your local symphony?

I also asked you to watch and see what makes you angry. Did you know that we can discover our dreams that way? For instance, perhaps you have seen on the news that public displays of the Ten Commandments are being removed all over the United States. Something rises up in you, saying, "That is not right!" Maybe you go so far as to write a letter in protest or otherwise express your disapproval. Your activism may be part of your destiny, part of your dream. God's dream for you may be for you to be a crusader for what's right, a voice for His cause, a champion of the faith in your city or your nation or the world.

I encourage you right now to think about your dreams and to begin the process of discovering what God's dreams for you might be, based on the information you've just read. Once you've identified your passions and giftings, submit those things to the Lord in prayer and allow the Holy Spirit to ignite one of them or some of them or all of them. Many women are gifted in several different areas and are passionate about a number of causes or situations. But passion and gifting together do not necessarily compose God's dream for your life. May I tell you something? God's anointing and His favor tend to accompany His dreams for your life. You can sense His anointing on an idea or a desire in prayer. As His anointing comes upon your prayer, you will sense a super-natural "charge" or a surge of passion or an impression of the Lord cheering you on in that area. Often, when you are praying under an anointing, the Holy Spirit will cause you to stretch and ask for more than you may be comfortable with—but He will also give you the faith to believe for it!

God will show you your destiny if you call out to Him. An intimate moment with Jesus will leave a burning sensation in your spirit for the rest of your life—and in one intimate moment, He can drop a dream in your heart, a dream that will take a lifetime to fulfill. You may not understand it at the time. It may be too great and too mighty for you, but if God calls you to a task, that means He takes the responsibility to equip you. The way you call out to Him is through prayer. To enter into a business decision, a marriage, a new adventure without seeking God first can be very dangerous. No matter how good it looks, always turn to God in prayer first!

> *An intimate moment with Jesus will leave a burning sensation in your spirit for the rest of your life—and in one intimate moment, He can drop a dream in your heart, a dream that will take a lifetime to fulfill.*

I have also mentioned that, along with an anointing, God's favor tends to accompany His dreams. If your dream is to get a college degree, look for His favor (that sense that He is "on your side," that He is making a way for you) as you begin to investigate schools and as you apply. His favor may be revealed to you in countless ways. For instance, it might be evident as you speak with admissions officers—you might just feel that one of them really likes you and sincerely wants to help. His favor may show up in the financial aid office, when you are offered more assistance at one school than at another.

You're On

1. What are you drawn to, interested in, or passionate for?

_____

_____

_____

_____

2. What are you willing to sacrifice or take risks for?

_____

_____

_____

_____

3. When you pray about your life and your future, what seems to be especially anointed as you commune with God?

_____

_____

_____

_____

> *If God calls you to a task, that means He takes the responsibility to equip you.*

Learn Your Lines

Call to Me, and I will answer you,
and show you great
and mighty things, which you do not know.
Jeremiah 33:3

Now we have received not the spirit of the world,
but the Spirit who is from God,
that we might know the things
that have been freely given to us by God.
1 Corinthians 2:12

Continue earnestly in prayer, being vigilant
in it with thanksgiving . . .
Colossians 4:2

Do not neglect the gift that is in you,
which was given to you
by prophecy with the
laying on of the hands
of the eldership.
Meditate on these things;
give yourself entirely to them,
that your progress may be evident to all.
1 Timothy 4:14, 15

*Let God
lead you into His
exciting, fulfilling
dreams for
your life.*

Coming Soon

*I*sn't it exciting to think about really knowing what God dreams of when He looks upon you? Isn't it wonderful to imagine yourself fully partnering with Him to bring those dreams into reality in your life? As you consider these things and look forward to fulfilling His plans and purposes, what's in your heart? Express your thoughts and hopes and feelings on the lines provided.

_____

_____

_____

_____

_____

_____

_____

_____

_____

_____

_____

_____

_____

ACTION!

*B*ased on what you have learned in this chapter, what are three concise, measurable, attainable goals you will set for yourself when it comes to letting go of your own agenda and embracing God's plans and purposes for you? One of your goals might be as simple as setting aside some prayer time to release any soulish dreams you have and to commit yourself to God's dreams for your life. Be sure to include a schedule and target date for reaching each goal and a reward for accomplishing it.

1. Goal: _____

Schedule and target completion date: _____

Reward: _____

_____

2. Goal: _____

Schedule and target completion date: _____

Reward: _____

_____

3. Goal: _____

Schedule and target completion date: _____

Reward: _____

_____

3

The Lady, the Dreamer

Introducing

I f you are going fulfill God's exciting destiny for your life and to see your dreams come true, you are going to have to know who you are and embrace your unique identity as a woman of God. You are going to have to resist the lies of the enemy and embrace who God says you are. You'll need to be so sure of His love for you that no challenge to your dream can threaten your position as His beloved daughter, and you'll need to be so certain of His calling on your life that no obstacle will make you want to give up. You have to be secure in your identity—not putting on a different mask for every person or situation you encounter, not hesitant about who you are or unable to express your personality for fear of what people might think. I encourage you to discover who you are as God's tailor-made leading lady and to celebrate your identity in Him!

The Main Event

Act 1: Who Is This Dreamer?

There is no one like you. You are fearfully and wonderfully made, which means that God precisely put you together, each intricate piece of you has been set in place by God. You are distinguished, marked and uniquely crafted by the hand of God Himself. He has perfectly, genetically, and distinctly put you together. You are the workmanship, or the product, of almighty God. You are specially designed, ordered, and delivered to be God's instrument in the earth. You are a rare artifact, a priceless treasure, an irreplaceable jewel. Your handprint cannot be duplicated. Your smile, your laugh, your voice will never be copied. You and your life have been planned according to His brilliant blueprint. You are the one and only you.

Do you realize that never before and never again will you be created? God made you specifically, at this time, in your family, your workplace, your city, your nation or your specific sphere of influence, to do something no one else can do.

You are not where you are today by accident; you are where you are by the divine plan of the sovereign God of this universe. Your purpose, your destiny, your future may be hidden from you now, but realize this, God will show you the mysteries of your life. You may be single, divorced, widowed, separated, violated, or abandoned; but if you will

> *If you are made by design, then that means the artist (God) knows your value. You are the canvas and He has the brush of destiny.*

surrender your life to the Lord, you will discover your destiny and see your dreams come true.

You are a leading lady, and I believe that God has transformed your life and produced the work of regeneration. So you can be confident that since God initiated your salvation and called you to a great destiny, then He will continue this work to its completion and cause you to accomplish His purposes for your life. Never forget that "He who has begun a good work in you will complete it until the day of Christ Jesus" (Phil. 1:6). Remember that God finished you before He started you; He knows exactly what you need in order to fulfill your dreams because He sees the end from the beginning.

Today, begin to thank God for one thing about yourself and go from there; because what you look at longest will eventually become your strongest.

Declare this out loud, "I have a destiny. I have a purpose that has been ordained by God. Starting today, I will look for those things, which have been assigned to my life before I was born. I cannot fail because I am a miracle in the making."

The Bible is full of scriptures that tell you who you are in Christ, and I want to declare some of them over you right now. These words are truth!

◆ You are victorious (Rev. 21:7).

◆ You are established to the end (1 Cor. 1:18).

◆ You are more than a conqueror (Rom. 8:37).

◆ You are an ambassador for Christ (2 Cor. 5:20).

◆ You are beloved of God (1 Thess. 1:4).

◆ You are overtaken with blessings (Deut. 28:2).

◆ You are complete in Christ (Col. 2:10).

◆ You are firmly rooted, built up and strengthened in the faith (Col. 2:7).

◆ You are always triumphant in Christ Jesus (2 Cor. 2:14).

You're On

1. Speaking out of the faith that is in you, who are you and what are you capable of?

You are always triumphant in Christ Jesus (2 Cor. 2:14)

2. What quality do you like most about yourself?

_____

_____

_____

_____

_____

_____

_____

_____

3. What area of your life do you feel needs the most improvement?

_____

_____

_____

_____

_____

_____

_____

_____

4. Of the confessions I have written about you, which one do you most need to personalize?

_____

_____

_____

_____

_____

_____

_____

5. What is it about yourself that you are going to thank God for today?

_____

_____

_____

_____

_____

_____

_____

Learn Your Lines

Instead of giving you specific Bible verses to learn, I'd like for you to look at the list of confessions that begin with "You are . . ." and read the Bible verses that are noted in parentheses next to each one. Choose 3 or 4 verses that you know you need to stand on, and memorize them. Write them in the spaces below.

_1._ _____

_____

_____

_____

_____

_____

_____

_2._ _____

_____

_____

_____

_____

_____

_____

3. _____

_____

_____

_____

_____

_____

_____

_____

_____

_____

4. _____

_____

_____

_____

_____

_____

_____

_____

_____

_____

_____

Act 2: Called, Chosen, Beloved

Now that I have stirred you up by proclaiming the Word over you and declaring who you are, I will list some confessions (based on Bible verses) for you below. I encourage you to read over these statements because they define who you really are. Choose several to really meditate on and repeat to yourself so that you can get the truth of the Word into your heart and be confident in the woman God created you to be.

◆ I am chosen and appointed by Christ to bear His fruit (John 15:16).

◆ I am a child of God; He is my spiritual Father (Rom. 8:14-15; Gal. 3:26; 4:6).

◆ I am free from condemnation (Rom. 8:1).

◆ I am a joint heir with Christ, sharing His inheritance with Him (Rom. 8:17).

◆ I am called according to God's purpose (Rom. 8:28).

◆ I am a temple, a dwelling place, of God. My body is the temple of the Holy Spirit (1 Cor. 3:16; 6:19).

◆ I am not my own, I have been bought with a price and I belong to God (1 Cor. 6:19, 20).

◆ I am established, anointed and sealed by God in Christ (2 Cor. 1:21, 22).

◆ I am a new creation in Christ (2 Cor. 5:17).

◆ I am the righteousness of God in Christ (2 Cor. 5:21).

◆ I am an heir of God through Christ because I am a child of God (Gal. 4:6, 7).

◆ I am blessed with every spiritual blessing (Eph. 1:3).

◆ I am accepted in the Beloved (Eph. 1:6).

◆ I am redeemed and forgiven, according to the riches of His grace (Eph. 1:7, 8).

◆ I am God's workmanship, created in Christ for good works (Eph. 2:10).

◆ I am a fellow citizen with the saints and members of God's family (Eph. 2:19).

◆ I am able to approach God with boldness and confidence through faith (Eph. 3:12).

◆ I am a citizen of heaven, seated in heavenly places in Christ Jesus (Phil. 3:20; Eph. 2:6).

◆ I am able to do all things through Christ who strengthens me (Phil. 4:13).

◆ I am hidden with Christ in God (Col. 3:3).

◆ I am chosen of God, holy and beloved (Col. 3:12).

◆ I am a daughter of light and not of darkness (1 Thess. 5:5).

◆ I am a holy partaker of a heavenly calling (Heb. 3:1).

◆ I am one of God's living stones, being built up in Christ as a spiritual house (1 Pet. 2:5).

◆ I am a member of a chosen generation, a royal priesthood, a holy nation, His own special people (1 Pet. 2:9).

Adapted from Neil Anderson's *Victory Over the Darkness* © 2000 by Neil T. Anderson, published by Regal Books, Ventura, CA.

You're On

1. As you read the list of confessions above, which ones are you already confident in?

_____

_____

_____

_____

2. Which confessions above are most challenging to you?

_____

_____

_____

_____

3. Will you commit to doing everything you can to get these truths about yourself deeply into your heart?

_____

_____

_____

_____

Learn Your Lines

Instead of giving you specific Bible verses to learn, I'd like for you to look at the list of "I am . . ." confessions above and choose 3 or 4 that are especially relevant to you. Then, look up the Bible verses that correspond to those confessions and memorize them. Write those verses in the spaces provided below.

1. _____

_____

_____

_____

_____

_____

2. _____

_____

_____

_____

_____

_____

3.

4.

COMING SOON

Can you imagine what it would be like to really know who you are and to walk in the fullness of everything God has created and called you to be? What lies of the enemy will be demolished as you walk in your true identity? Use the space below to journal some of the vision you are gaining for your life as you realize what a unique and valuable woman you are.

_____

_____

_____

_____

_____

_____

_____

_____

_____

_____

_____

_____

_____

_____

_____

ACTION!

*B*ased on what you have learned in this chapter, what are three concise, measurable, attainable goals you will set for yourself in the area of your identity in Christ and being confident in who God made you so that you can boldly pursue your dreams? Be sure to include a schedule and target date for reaching each goal and a reward for accomplishing it.

1. Goal: _____

Schedule and target completion date: _____

Reward: _____

_____

2. Goal: _____

Schedule and target completion date: _____

Reward: _____

_____

3. Goal: _____

Schedule and target completion date: _____

Reward: _____

_____

4

The Lady Looks Ahead

Introducing

n order to fulfill God's dreams for your life, one of the first things you will need to do is to put the pain of your past behind you. There are elements of your past that have been God's intentional training ground for your future, but there have also been aspects of your past that were sent from the pit of hell to try to steal, kill, and destroy God's plans and purposes for your life. Going forward, you need to glean what has been good and deal with the rest so that the chains of past failures, hurts and disappointments do not hold you back as you head toward everything God has for you.

In this chapter, I'd like to help you begin to deal with the wounds of the past, get healed, be set free, and embrace the dreams that are waiting for you in God.

The Main Event

Act 1: Put the Pain Behind You

I have observed, through years in ministry, that the number one issue that prevents people from going forward in their walk with God and fulfilling His dreams for their lives is unforgiveness. Many Christians miss out on their blessing because they choose not to forgive and forget the painful things that have happened to them. When we choose to walk in unforgiveness, we become trapped in our past, we become blinded, we become powerless and we become a target for the enemy because we are in agreement with him.

I realize that certain situations in your life may have been heartbreaking or tragic. But even in the wake of terrible injustices or sins against you, you must forgive—otherwise those situations will control you for the rest of your life. You do not have to carry your pain. By holding on to it, you are telling God you can handle it. You are forgiven from your past, so do not revisit it in your mind. The more you think about your past, the more you talk about your past, the more you will remember your past. Satan wants you to visit your past to bring you under condemnation. If you fall into his trap, you will lose your joy, your shout, and your victory.

But God wants you to be healed from the pain of the past and to move on into a bright future; and He knows that you

> *God wants you to be healed from the pain of the past and to move on into a bright future; and He knows that you must forgive those who have hurt you if you are going to fulfill your destiny.*

must forgive those who have hurt you if you are going to fulfill your destiny. He demands forgiveness for your benefit. You can only be free from your transgressors by allowing God to do what only He can do—forgive the unforgivable.

Forgiveness is not only difficult, it is humanly impossible. We take the first step by recognizing our need to forgive. We take the second step by realizing that we do not have the ability to forgive in our own strength. Then, by asking God to fill us with His love and make us forgive, we are cleansed of the bitter poison in our soul, and we can walk back into the light, seeing His will on the perfect pathway to peace.

Once you have forgiven, then forget. Forget the offense and let go of the pain. The apostle Paul writes in Philippians 3:13, 14: ". . . one thing I do, forgetting those things which are behind and reaching forward to those things which are ahead, I press toward the goal for the prize of the upward call of God in Christ Jesus." He shares with us that he has not yet "arrived," but that there is one thing that is imperative for him to do: in order to go forth he must forget the past. He must let go of all his yesterdays. Whether yesterday was good or bad, he must release it.

You cannot enter your tomorrow as long as you hold on to your past. You must let it go.

Like Paul, you cannot enter your tomorrow as long as you hold on to your past. You must let it go. I know, that's easier said than done. Your past may contain brokenness, disappointment, and scars from life's tragedies. So what will it take to let it go? Are you ready to have a funeral, bury your past? Your tomorrow does not need to end up like your yesterdays. In fact, it is a tragedy to plan your future by comparing it to your past! I encourage you from my own experience: Stop using what happened to you before to determine what will happen in your future.

> *You have a future, and you are the one whom God has picked to go for it. So move on with God.*

Where you came from does not determine where you are going. That is good news for many of us. Too many people have predicted their ending by their beginning. Let God interrupt your life and change the course of history in your life for the good. He does not want you to live in the past and grieve over what has not happened or what has been lost. It is dangerous to hold onto things that need to be released. Too many times we miss our destiny because we stay in the past. Do not let anyone hold you back or to make you a prisoner of your past. Remember, you have become a new creation in Christ. What you have gone through is for His glory, and at the right time, Jesus will shine through you. You have a future, and you are the one whom God has picked to go for it. So move on with God.

You're On

1. Is there any unforgiveness in your heart?

_____

_____

_____

_____

_____

_2._ Can you see how unforgiveness is keeping you from moving on with God?

_3._ Specifically, who, or what, do you need to forgive? (You can forgive them using the prayer below).

_4._ Are you ready to forgive the people who have hurt you? Are you ready to let go of the unforgiveness that is robbing you of your destiny? Then pray this prayer with me:

"Father, place within my heart forgiveness toward anyone who has hurt me, wronged me, or caused harm against me. I release them and declare they are forgiven and I am free."

5. What aspects of your past do you need to forget and release in order to be free to fulfill your dreams?

_____

_____

_____

_____

_____

_____

_____

_____

_____

The same God who saved you, called you. The God who called you, gifted you; and He has a perfect place and a position in life for you. Choose today to embrace the dream and to walk out the divine plan of God for your life.

Learn Your Lines

For if you forgive men their trespasses,
your heavenly Father will also forgive you.
But if you do not forgive men their trespasses,
neither will your Father forgive your trespasses.
Matthew 6:14, 15

Then Peter came to Him and said, "Lord,
how often shall my brother sin against me,
and I forgive him? Up to seven times?"
Jesus said to him, "I do not say to you,
up to seven times,
but up to seventy times seven."
Matthew 18:21, 22

And be kind to one another, tenderhearted,
forgiving one another, even
as God in Christ forgave you.
Ephesians 4:32

But I press on, that I may lay hold of that
for which Christ Jesus has also laid hold of me…
one thing I do, forgetting those things which
are behind and reaching forward to those
things which are ahead, I press toward the
goal for the prize of the upward call of
God in Christ Jesus.
Philippians 3:12-14

Act 2: Embrace the Dream

Your greatest days are ahead of you because God's mercy and compassion do not fail. They are new every morning. Instead of looking back to last year and reminiscing about the things you may not have accomplished, remember this: God is ready to renew you each morning with His favor to fulfill your destiny. Your past cannot stop you. Your failures cannot stop you. Your shortcomings cannot stop you. Why? Because God is a merciful God, and He is faithful. So, no matter what has happened, you can embrace your dream today.

I am so excited about God's plan for your life! You know, He has a plan for each and every person. Some abort their plan; others avoid their plan; but you must embrace the dream inside of you and accept His plan to achieve your God-given goals. He has a detailed desire for your success.

Your greatest days are ahead of you because God's mercy and compassion do not fail.

If you have not opened your arms wide to receive His dream for your life, then the only thing stopping its fulfillment is you. I am telling you, excuses cannot stop the plan of God. Satan cannot stop the plan of God. Calamity cannot stop the plan of God. Disease cannot stop the plan of God. Nothing—absolutely nothing—can stop the will of God but your will. Choose today to reflect on what God has promised you, not on what you have done up to this point. The same God who saved you, called you. The God who called you, gifted you; and He has a perfect place and a position in life for you. Choose today to embrace the dream and to walk out the divine plan of God for your life. Say aloud, "I will bless the Lord and forget not any of His benefits. I will walk in His steps and do His will."

Every one of us has the same amount of time afforded us to determine how far we will go in the things of God. If we do not fulfill what God has purposed for us, then we cannot say we have really lived. Each of us is responsible for the distance we will go with God and for saying "Yes!" to embracing and fulfilling the dream He has for us. Only those who risk going too far will ever know how far they can go. I tell you that if you can see the invisible, you can do the impossible. Your only boundaries are your perception of your potential. As you embrace your dream, give yourself a picture of your potential. Just keep seeing yourself fulfilling that dream and leaping over every hurdle that would stand in the way of your destiny.

No matter what may try to hinder you, Jesus spoke a powerful word over your situation because He wants to see your dreams come true. He declared, "It is finished!"

No matter what may try to hinder you, Jesus spoke a powerful word over your situation because He wants to see your dreams come true. He declared, "It is finished!" (John 19:30). What does that mean for you right now? It means that everything you need in order to fulfill your destiny, He has supplied. For every trial, He has already prayed; and every battle He has already won. You can embrace God's plans and purposes of your life with confidence because His Word is provisionary, powerful, and prophetic. Just receive it, say "Yes!" to Him and embrace your dream!

You're On

1. Are you embracing God's dream for your life? If not, what's holding you back?

_____

_____

_____

_____

2. What are you doing to advance God's purposes in your life right now?

_____

_____

_____

_____

3. What can you do in the near future to more completely embrace and walk out God's destiny for you?

_____

_____

_____

_____

Learn Your Lines

Delight yourself also in the Lord, and He shall give you the desires of your heart.

Psalm 37:4

That good thing which was committed to you, keep by the Holy Spirit who dwells in us.

2 Timothy 1:14

. . . let us lay aside every weight, and the sin which so easily ensnares us, and let us run with endurance the race that is set before us.

Hebrews 12:1

Each of us is responsible for the distance we will go with God and for saying "Yes!" to embracing and fulfilling the dream He has for us.

COMING SOON

*H*ave you ever tasted the freedom that comes with true forgiveness? If not, take my word for it: it's really great. It will liberate and empower you to pursue your dreams with intensity and a freshness you may not have experienced before. What kind of hopes and aspirations do you have for yourself as you enjoy the power of forgiveness? What are you going to leave behind as you walk into a new life, free to fulfill all His purposes for you? How are you going to embrace God's destiny for your life?

ACTION!

*B*ased on what you have learned in this chapter, what are three concise, measurable, attainable goals you will set for yourself when it comes to putting the past behind you and embracing God's dreams for your life? Be sure to include a schedule and target date for reaching each goal and a reward for accomplishing it.

1. Goal: _____

Schedule and target completion date: _____

Reward: _____

_____

2. Goal: _____

Schedule and target completion date: _____

Reward: _____

_____

3. Goal: _____

Schedule and target completion date: _____

Reward: _____

_____

5

The Lady Is Right on Time

Introducing

eading ladies are full of power and grace, right? I'm not just talking about having influence around the table in the boardroom or having Holy Ghost power to cast out demons. And I'm not just talking about the grace with which you move as you make your way around a room in your elegant dress with your manicured nails and your perfectly set hair. I'm not even talking about the grace to be nice to someone who has offended you. No, I am talking about another kind of power and an uncommon kind of grace. I am talking about a true challenge—the power and the grace to wait.

Waiting on God is not popular when it must be applied personally. Oh, we don't mind encouraging someone else to wait on Him or to "stand still and see the salvation of the Lord," but when we have to wait—well, that's different! But sister, there is no way around it. If you are going to fulfill your destiny in God and see those dreams come true, you are going to have to do it His way—and on His timetable. You've heard it before, but I'll remind you: His timing is perfect. No matter how you may struggle as you wait on Him, you'll eventually see that He was never late in your life. He won't be early either, but give yourself to the rhythm of His timing in your life; you're going to end up realizing that He is—and therefore, you are—always right on time.

The Main Event

Act 1: God's Got the Clock

God will place you at the right place at the right time to meet the right person to open the right door. He knows how old you are; He knows how long you've been waiting; He knows how eager you are for the next season of your life to come forth in full bloom. He is the master puppeteer who is making all the right moves, orchestrating each event that comes your way, preparing your blessing, stumbling your way—as Ruth did—into Boaz' field, which symbolizes the place of fulfilled destiny (Ruth 2:2). And He is doing everything that concerns you in His perfect time.

If you are going to fulfill your destiny in God and see those dreams come true, you are going to have to do it His way—and on His timetable.

I know, it's easier said than done, but you must realize that God holds the clock of your life and in order to cooperate with Him, you'll have to submit to His timing. It isn't always easy, but I guarantee it's always best.

Submitting to God's timing will require at least two things of you: trust and humility. The Bible says: "But they that wait upon the Lord. . . shall mount up with wings as eagles" (Is. 40:31). The Hebrew word for wait means, "to wait with hopeful expectancy." I think of this as trusting with unlimited confidence. Isaiah is not saying "wait," in reference to time. He is not writing about a time issue, but about trusting God. It takes trust in order to flow with God's timing in your life. You see, if you focus on time and on how long you have been waiting for such-and-such to happen, you will lose sight of God's big picture and you will get frustrated. But if you focus on trusting, then timing becomes less important because you are confident that everything will happen exactly when it should, according to God's wisdom and plan.

When you learn to trust with unlimited confidence, the Lord will renew your strength. God knows when it is the right time for you to go forward, and He knows when you are ready. You may not know how or when, but in due season, God will thrust you out to reach your destiny. Like the young eagle soaring for the first time, you can also soar to new horizons in God when you fully trust Him. Leading lady, you can soar like an eagle; just trust Him for the perfect timing.

I wrote to you that not only will you need to trust God in His timing, but that you will also need to exercise humility. Trusting Him demands humility—because you must put aside all of your pride and your own agenda and simply rest in God. The

> *God knows when it is the right time for you to go forward, and He knows when you are ready. You may not know how or when, but in due season, God will thrust you out to reach your destiny*

apostle Peter (who was not exactly known for his patience!) makes an interesting observation about the connection between humility and God's timing. He writes: "Therefore humble yourselves under the mighty hand of God, that He may exalt you in due time" (1 Pet. 5:6). This phrase "in due time" is important to understand. In the Greek, it means, "set or proper" time. In other words, if you are willing to humble yourself, or go through the process, and wait on the Lord, then God Himself will exalt you. God will do this; it is His promise to you. But remember this: it will happen at a pre-set time.

In fact, there is a set time for every event in your life. Everything God does is scheduled. Everything is to happen in its time. Maybe you have been waiting for that certain job, car, mate, or finances. Just hold on. Your breakthrough has been scheduled before time. Do not try to force what God has set for that "certain" time.

> *Maybe you have been waiting for that certain job, car, mate, or finances. Just hold on. Your breakthrough has been scheduled before time. Do not try to force what God has set for that "certain" time.*

What happens if you are too impatient to wait for God's time? When you are too impatient to wait for the promise of God, you will begin to strive and try to work things out in your own flesh. When that happens, you often create a whole new set of problems. So start your day by telling God you are willing and ready, but want Him to have His way with you—whenever He sees fit. The Spirit knows where you need to go—and when you need to go—in order to be victorious as you fulfill God's dreams for your life.

You're On

1. In what areas of your life have you been impatient in the past? What has been the result? (Now would be a good time to repent and to tell the Lord you embrace His timing from now on).

The Spirit knows where you need to go — and when you need to go — in order to be victorious as you fulfill God's dreams for your life.

2. How have you moved out of humble trust in the past and tried to rush God's purposes in your life? When have you worked in the flesh to try and accomplish what only God can do? (Repent for those activities and surrender to the Spirit's working in your life from now on).

---

3. In what areas of your life are you currently struggling with God's timing? What do you feel you have waited "forever" for? (Again, repent for not embracing God's schedule for you, and thank Him that, even though you may not understand, you are right in the center of His will for you.)

_____

_____

_____

_____

_____

_____

_____

Learn Your Lines

But as for me, I trust in You, O Lord; I say,
"You are my God."
My times are in Your hands.
Psalm 31:14, 15

Your eyes saw my substance, being yet unformed.
And in Your book they were all written,
the days fashioned for me, when as
yet there were none of them.
Psalm 139:16

But those who wait on the Lord shall
renew their strength;
they shall mount up with wings like eagles,
they shall run and
not be weary,
they shall walk and not faint.
Isaiah 40:31

To everything there is a season,
a time for every purpose under heaven.
Ecclesiastes 3:1

He has made everything beautiful in its time . . .
Ecclesiastes 3:11a

Act 2: Am I There Yet?

I've got great news for you: Where you are is not where you are going to be. There is a place in God that He wants you to go to, but in order to get there and to handle both the blessings and the responsibilities God will give you in that place, you must go through a season of preparation. I need to warn you that your time of preparation may not be the most fun season of your life. It may be grueling and intense—but only in proportion to the greatness of God's dream for your life. And I will assure you, if you start asking whether or not you have reached a destiny moment without a season of preparation, the answer is no. You are not there yet! God's preparation always precedes His promises!

When Jesus started His ministry, He too went through a time of preparation—40 days in the wilderness, without a

> *Where you are is not where you are going to be.*

bite to eat! The Spirit led Him into the wilderness (in other words, it was all part of God's plan) and while He there, He was tempted by the devil. Jesus was alone, but He was not lonely. He was separated for a purpose. It was a season of *separation* for a season of *preparation*. Your season of separation is just that—a season. But do not get confused in its purpose; it is to prepare you for your calling. God is preparing you for your career, your business, your family, your future and your destiny. Remember that, and keep the dream always before you. The preparation is not your destination; your destiny is.

Seasons of preparation are almost always characterized by testings and trials. God doesn't need us to prove to Him that we can pass the tests necessary to move on into the promises He's given us; He knows that we need to know we can pass them. The apostle Paul, who knew many sufferings and trials, wrote these words about difficult times and circumstances: " . . .we also glory in tribulations, knowing that tribulation produces perseverance; and perseverance, character; and character, hope" (Rom. 5:3). The word translated *glory* in English is doxa in the Greek; and it means "God's praise" or "God's integrity." When Paul said we "glory in tribulations," he meant that despite what comes our way, we can go through it with peace, with joy and with Gods arms wrapped around us. God does His most powerful work when we are weak, empty and helpless. That is the state we do not like to be in, but it is the condition out of which God builds masterpieces. In those places, we see His integrity, and from them, we sing His praises.

> *To have a testimony (which is your destiny story), you must first go through a test.*

To have a testimony (which is your destiny story), you must first go through a test. What looks like a mess is your make-up for a miracle. For supernatural glory to be manifested, you must realize that your testing is not for your benefit alone, but for His glory to be made known in you.

James wrote: "My brethren, count it all joy when you fall into various trials, knowing that the testing of your faith produces patience" (James 1:2, 3). In the beautiful King James Version of the Bible, the word "temptations" is used in this verse, in place of "trials." In this context, it does not refer to a temptation by the devil. The Greek word can also be translated, "trial or testing." This test is put in your life to draw you to God, not push you away. Pressure is a good thing; testing is a good thing. It is a driving force that the Lord will use to get you where He wants you. Your trials are not intended to make you fail or fall. They are intended to make you more like Christ.

What was meant to destroy you can actually be what makes you strong and whole. What was supposed to be a stumbling block in your life can actually become a stepping-stone.

So how can James tell us to "count it all joy" when we go through trials and when our faith is tested? This "testing" is not what you may think. Interestingly, the Greek word used in James 1:3 refers to "an opportunity in life." It is a chance to prove the faithfulness of God. It is a chance to persevere and to demonstrate God's faithfulness. It gives you the opportunity to pass the test, come out stronger, and give God the praise.

When we pass the test, we mature and become complete; we are "lacking nothing," according to James 4:4. The test is only a stepping-stone to your next destination with God. It becomes the ladder to your impossibilities. It becomes the stairway to your abundance. What was meant to destroy you can actually be what makes you strong and whole. What was supposed to be a stumbling block in your life can actually become a stepping-stone.

Leading lady, good, solid, deep preparation is essential for you. I believe God has big dreams for your life—great purposes and grand plans that would blow your mind if you fully understood them right now. And in order to stand firm and to walk strong in everything He has, you've got to be prepared.

> *I believe God has big dreams for your life—great purposes and grand plans that would blow your mind if you fully understood them right now.*

You're On

1. What testings and trials are you encountering right now on your journey toward destiny?

_____

_____

_____

_____

2. Are you counting your various trials "all joy?" If not, I suggest you repent and then change your tune!

_____

_____

_____

_____

_____

_____

3. According to what you have read in this chapter, what are some of the reasons we encounter testings and trials?

_____

_____

_____

_____

_____

_____

Learn Your Lines

*And we know that all things work together
for good to those who love God,
to those who are called according to His purpose.*
Romans 8:28

*Therefore be patient, brethren, until the
coming of the Lord. See how the farmer
waits for the precious fruit of the earth,
waiting patiently for it until it
receives the early and the latter rain.*
James 5:7

*But may the God of all grace, who called
us to His eternal glory by Christ Jesus,
after you have suffered a while, perfect,
establish, strengthen, and settle you.*
1 Peter 5:10

*If you are
going to fulfill
your destiny in God
and see those dreams come
true, you are going to have
to do it His way--and on
His timetable.*

COMING SOON

 know, I know, when you see the words "Coming Soon," you may have said to yourself, "I sure hope the end of this season of testing is coming soon!" But I urge you to look beyond then. Can you discern the purposes of God during this time of preparation? Has He revealed to you why He is training you the way He is? What good can come of the preparation you are going through? How can He be glorified? Now that's something good to think about coming soon!

ACTION!

*B*ased on what you have learned in this chapter, what are three concise, measurable, attainable goals you will set for yourself when it comes to trusting God's timing and maximizing your seasons of preparation? Be sure to include a schedule and target date for reaching each goal and a reward for accomplishing it.

1. Goal: _____

Schedule and target completion date: _____

Reward: _____

_____

2. Goal: _____

Schedule and target completion date: _____

Reward: _____

_____

3. Goal: _____

Schedule and target completion date: _____

Reward: _____

_____

6

The Lady Lives by the Word

Introducing

You are a leading lady and as such, you've set standards for yourself. You have personal standards, social standards, standards for your work and standards for the way you look. I hope you also uphold a standard of truth in your life, and that the Word of God is that standard against which you measure every thought, every feeling, every relationship, every crisis, every opportunity and every situation you encounter.

Each day in our Christian journey, God has something new for us to learn. There is a Word from heaven waiting for every hungry heart each time we dive into the Bible. I cannot download to you all the riches and all the power of the Word; you have to discover them for yourself. I want to share with you, in this chapter, how powerful the Word is and to urge you to read, study and meditate on the Scriptures for yourself so that you will be transformed and your life will be changed for the better. The only firm foundation on which to build a successful life is the Word of God, and I believe with all my heart that your life depends on it.

The Main Event

Act 1: There's Power in the Word

We cannot underestimate the power of the Word. It really does have the power to change your life. God's Word is like rain and snow saturating the soil to produce a harvest. His Word created the galaxies, the earth, sun and moon. It is the most powerful source in the world today. When things stand in your way and try to prevent you from reaching the destiny God has for you, His Word smashes those roadblocks away. God's Word will keep your thoughts in check when your flesh wants to chase something that is not good for you; and it will protect you when your eyes see something that would put you in harm's way.

Furthermore, the Word separates you from the world and consecrates you for service. As Jesus said in John 17:17, God's Word is truth. You know what truth does—it confronts and obliterates the lies the devil has told you. It keeps you from being deceived. The more you apply the Word to your life, the more you receive an anointing to walk in truth. When truth is revealed, joy is discovered. When joy is discovered, strength is deposited.

> *I hope you also uphold a standard of truth in your life, and that the Word of God is that standard against which you measure every thought, every feeling and every situation you encounter.*

When you touch the Word, it makes you whole. It makes you free. It heals the body, the mind, the emotions, the memories and every issue of life. When the Word is absent from your lips, miracles are missing. Your strength is lacking, and your direction is veiled like a mystery.

When God's Word is present, His will is known. God will show you what His will is. Your vision, your destiny, your future is within you. Yes, I said within you. The Word is in you, but for you to know your future, you must know the Word.

Once you know God's will and have it confirmed in heart by the Word, the enemy will try to keep you from walking in it. He will tempt you, but the Word also gives you power to overcome discouragement and temptation and to stand against the enemy (who is out to kill your dreams— remember?). When you are faced with temptation, the devil will begin to talk to your soul realm, so you will have to win your battles with the weapon of the Word. I am reminded of the prophet Jeremiah, who fell into despair and was tempted to give up. He found himself frustrated numerous times in his ministry because the people refused to listen to his words and heed his urgent warnings. But even in his deepest day of discouragement, he said, "His word was in my heart like a burning fire shut up in my bones" (Jer. 20:9)

I believe Jeremiah was saying, in essence, "When I cannot go any further, the Word pushes me. When I think I am going to quit and give up, the Word gives me fortitude. When everyone opposes me and I want to walk away, the

> *The more you apply the Word to your life, the more you receive an anointing to walk in truth. When truth is revealed, joy is discovered. When joy is discovered, strength is deposited.*

Word turns me around and causes me to walk back into confrontation for the cause of the kingdom." That's the power of the Word—and like Jeremiah, you are called of God and appointed for a holy purpose and you need to be saturated with the Word so that it can strengthen and compel you and push you on to victory as you fulfill your destiny in God.

There is a spiritual assault coming from the corridors of hell—it's headed straight for the dream inside of you, so you need to fortify yourself with strong spiritual ammunition and know how to wield the weapon of the Word.

There is a spiritual assault coming from the corridors of hell—it's headed straight for the dream inside of you, so you need to fortify yourself with strong spiritual ammunition and know how to wield the weapon of the Word. The closer you get to God, the greater threat you are to hell. The enemy does not take a day off or rest for a minute. You are not to be ignorant or unaware of his plans against you. The best defense is to have a plan for yourself; and that plan is to know your weapon—the sword of the Spirit, which is the Word of God.

Allow the Word of God to penetrate your soul, your mind and your spirit. Do not let your present circumstances dictate your potential future. Bring the life-changing power of God's Word to bear on your situation. Get in the Word and speak your future today. Your dreams depend on it!

You're On

1. According to what you have just read, what does the Word have the power to do in your life?

_____

_____

_____

_____

_____

_____

2. What do you most need the Word to do in your life? Help you overcome temptation? Set you free? Heal your mind or emotions? Help you guard your thoughts?

_____

_____

_____

_____

_____

_____

When the Word is absent from your lips, miracles are missing.

3. What does the Word do to the lies and assaults of the enemy? Are you personally appropriating its power?

The Word of God is a seed in your life. That seed needs to be watered, nurtured, and cultivated to fulfill its purpose.

Learn Your Lines

*The law of the Lord is perfect, converting
the soul; the testimony of the Lord is sure,
making wise the simple.*

Psalm 19:7

*Your word is a lamp unto my feet and
a light to my path.*

Psalm 119:105

*Every word of God is pure;
He is a shield to those
who put their trust in Him.*

Proverbs 30:5

*The grass withers, the flower fades,
but the word of our God stands forever.*

Isaiah 40:8

*For the word of God is living and powerful,
and sharper than any two-edged sword,
piercing even to the division of soul and spirit,
and of joints and marrow,
and is a discerner of the thoughts
and intents of the heart.*

Hebrews 4:12

Act 2: How to Work the Word

Everything in your spiritual walk comes back to a seed. The Word of God is a seed in your life. That seed needs to be watered, nurtured, and cultivated to fulfill its purpose. I urge you to read His Word and capture the promises of God in your heart. When you capture God's Word every day, you are feeding your spirit man, gaining strength for each new day. In fact, the apostle Peter compares the Word to milk for newborn babies. It is crucial for growth and life. He writes: "As new-born babes, desire the pure milk of the word, that you may grow thereby" (1 Pet. 2:2). Don't allow your busy schedule, influences for the world, or old friends to cause you to take for granted your desperate need to drink the milk of the Word.

Now you know that it is possible to hold a book in front of you and let your eyes pass over the words on a page without really comprehending what they mean. Your interaction with the Word needs to include not only reading what it says, but also grasping what it means and how it applies to your life. That will require you to *meditate* on the Word. The Hebrew word for *meditate* carries the connotation and the image of a cow chewing its cud. *Meditate*, in its original Hebrew (*hagah*), means also "to reflect," "to mutter (repeatedly)," "to ponder" or "to utter a thought out loud." Keep repeating the Word; say it to yourself; encourage yourself verbally with Bible verses. Like the cow with its cud, "chew" on the Word in your heart and in your mind until you are able to fully ingest and digest what it says to you. Only then will the Word nourish you, strengthen you, change you, and release its full benefit in your life.

God also gave Joshua a commandment as a promise to encourage and strengthen him. It was God's formula for success and it was to meditate on the Word.

Immediately following the death of Moses, Joshua became the leader of the children of Israel—a daunting task indeed! Obviously, Joshua was apprehensive, because four times in Joshua 1, God told him not to fear or be discouraged. But God also gave a Joshua a commandment as a promise to encourage and strengthen him. It was God's formula for success and it was to meditate on the Word. Read what He said:

> *When you capture God's Word every day, you are feeding your spirit man, gaining strength for each new day.*

> *This Book of the Law shall not depart from your mouth, but you shall meditate in it day and night, that you may observe to do according to all that is written in it. For then you will make your way prosperous, and then you will have good success. (Joshua 1:8)*

By studying the Word and meditating, you can learn about God and what He is capable of doing on your behalf. Through that consistent mind-renewing process, your expectation expands. And the more you know, the more faith grows, the more your life is changed and the more you advance in the fulfillment of your destiny.

There are several resources available to you as you learn to study the Word, understand it and meditate on it. These include: study Bibles, devotional Bibles, Bible commentaries, concordances, Bible dictionaries, Bible encyclopedias. I cannot encourage you strongly enough to invest in your study of the Word. I've already shared with you how powerful the Word is; and it will make such a difference in your life. God's Word is truth (John 17:17)—and the truth will set you free (John 8:32) to fulfill God's great dreams for your life.

You're On

1. What does it mean to "meditate on the Word"?

_____

_____

_____

2. Will you pick one Scripture to meditate on this week, to memorize and repeat over and over until it gets down deep into your heart and begins to change your life? Which one will you use?

_____

_____

_____

3. Do you need to purchase any of the Bible study resources listed above? Which ones? And when will you do so?

_____

_____

_____

Learn Your Lines

Let the word of Christ dwell in you richly in all wisdom,
teaching and admonishing one another in psalms
and hymns and spiritual songs,
singing with grace in your hearts to the Lord.
Colossians 3:16

For this reason we also thank God without ceasing,
because when you received the word of God
which you heard from us, you welcomed it
not as the word of men, but as it is in truth, the word of God,
which also effectively works in you who believe.
1 Thessalonians 2:13

Be diligent to present yourself approved to God,
a worker who does not need to be ashamed,
rightly dividing the word of truth.
2 Timothy 2:15

All Scripture is given by inspiration of God,
and is profitable for doctrine, for reproof, for correction,
for instruction in righteousness, that the man of God may
be complete, thoroughly equipped for every good work.
2 Timothy 3:16, 17

COMING SOON

*T*think you can tell by now how much I believe in the power of God's Word to change your life. As the Word begins to do its transforming work in you, how do you see your life changing as you align with God's truth? What do you think the Word will help you overcome? In what areas of struggle do you expect it to bring victory? What changes can you envision in yourself as you become rooted and grounded in the Scriptures?

ACTION!

*B*ased on what you have learned in this chapter, what are three concise, measurable, attainable goals you will set for yourself as you learn to live by the Word? Your goals might be to read the Bible every day, to increase your daily Bible reading, to begin a systematic program of Bible study or to memorize a verse per week. Be sure to include a schedule and target date for reaching each goal and a reward for accomplishing it.

1. Goal: _____

Schedule and target completion date: _____

Reward: _____

_____

2. Goal: _____

Schedule and target completion date: _____

Reward: _____

_____

3. Goal: _____

Schedule and target completion date: _____

Reward: _____

_____

7

The Lady Renews Her Mind

Introducing

Changing your world starts with changing your mind. Let me reiterate that: God has already given you the ability to change your world, and it starts by changing your mind. The mind is that which perceives, thinks, feels, wills, and desires. It conjures up your thoughts and deploys them into action; it takes you from the intangible to the tangible, from abstract to reality, from concept to implementation, from thought to experience—so your dream begins in your mind. That's why it is so important that your thinking be in alignment with the Word of God and that your mind is free from the influence of the world.

Romans 12:2 urges us: "And do not be conformed to this world, but be transformed by the renewing of your mind, that you may prove what is that good and perfect and acceptable will of God." Renewing your mind is like renovating a house. You will have to get rid of what's old in order to enjoy what's new. Old thought patterns will have to be stripped, like outdated wallpaper, before new ones can stick. The renewing of your mind is a process; it will not happen overnight. It will require conscious effort and work on your part. But I'll tell you—it's worth it. As Proverbs 23:7 teaches, we become what we think—and I know you want to become everything God has designed you to be. Your transformation starts in the mind.

The Main Event

Act 1: The Connection between Thoughts and Destiny

When teaching about the mind, I like to use a medical metaphor and say that the mind is the placenta of the spirit man. Your mind is what holds and nurtures the seeds of your destiny with which it has been impregnated until it is time for them to be delivered. You want to make sure that your dream is held in a safe place, don't you? You want it to be nourished by thoughts that agree with God's truth, don't you? Then you will have to make sure that your thoughts line up with His Word.

Your unique thinking is what separates you from other individuals, but if your thoughts, philosophies, ideas or reasoning are built on anything but the Word of God, they are nothing but sinking sand. They will not last. They will not produce the promises God has guaranteed in His Word. Thoughts that are contrary to God's Word will make you forfeit your destiny by causing you to live in bondage to them. That's right; the things that hinder so many people and keep them from reaching all God has for them all begin

> *God has already given you the ability to change your world, and it starts by changing your mind.*

as thoughts—fear, doubt, low self-esteem, depression, pride, and others.

That's why it is so important that you get rid of your old ways of thinking and build a new thought process based upon the Word of God. If you don't want depression, then you cannot continue to rehearse the same sickening thoughts that made you depressed in the first place. Tell the devil, "I'm changing my mind." Begin to align your thoughts with God's; you'll find them in His Word.

To align yourself with Christ and your thoughts with God's thoughts, you have to reprogram or renew your mind—move it from that problematic position into one that relates to the Word of God. You must become a student of the Word if you are serious about acquiring the mind of Christ. Once you know what the Word says, then you can think according to the truth that is in it.

> *You must become a student of the Word if you are serious about acquiring the mind of Christ. Once you know what the Word says, then you can think according to the truth that is in it.*

A great Bible verse to memorize as you renew your mind according to the Word is 2 Timothy 1:7, which tells us that God gives us a sound mind. The Greek word for "sound mind" means, in English, "discipline," or "self-control." This tells me that God has given you the discipline and self-control to stop negative, destructive, derogatory thoughts. You simply have to exercise that God-given ability. One way to do that is to memorize Philippians 4:8 (it's printed for you below in "Learn Your Lines" and to use it as the standard by which you measure your thoughts. It tells you exactly what kind of things to think about—things that are true, noble, just, pure, lovely, of good report, virtuous, and praise-worthy.

Your mind is a powerful thing. Unfortunately, most people never get their mind to work for them; instead, they get their mind to work against them—creating things they don't want. You unconsciously attract what you think you deserve. But as I wrote to you in the introduction to this chapter, you can change things by changing the way you think. If you don't like where you are, if you don't like the opportunities you have, if you don't like your environment or the atmosphere around your life, then change your thinking.

There is both potential treasure and potential trouble in the recesses of the mind.

There is no way to successfully reach your destiny in God without nourishing your dreams with positive, encouraging, empowering thoughts that are based on the Word. If you need some help getting started, go back and look at the chapter entitled, "The Lady Lives by the Word," because it will remind you of the power of the Word in your life.

As you accept the challenge to renew your mind as part of fulfilling your dreams, remember these often-repeated phrases:

Your thoughts become your words.
Your words become your actions.
Your actions become your habits.
Your habits become your character.
Your character becomes your destiny.

You're On

1. If the thoughts you are thinking today will ultimately become your destiny, are you on the right path?

_____

_____

_____

_____

Your dream begins in your mind.

2. What thoughts do you need to change in order to align with God's dreams for your life?

_____

_____

_____

_____

3. Are you renewing your mind according to the Word? If not, what will you do in order to start?

_____

_____

_____

_____

_____

Learn Your Lines

For as he thinks in his heart, so is he.
Proverbs 23:7

Finally, brethren, whatever things are true,
whatever things are noble,
whatever things are just,
whatever things are pure,
whatever things are lovely,
whatever things are of good report,
if there is any virtue and
if there is anything praiseworthy—
meditate on these things.
Philippians 4:8

For God has not given us a spirit of fear,
but of power and of love and of a sound mind.
2 Timothy 1:7

Act 2: Five Steps to Renewing Your Mind

1. Become aware of how you really think and what you really believe. What you believe is reality to you. Who you are in this world and who you will become boils down to the set of beliefs you have about yourself, and those beliefs— real or imagined—set up and define your self-concept, which greatly impacts your ability to fulfill your destiny. Therefore, you must face and deal with whatever you have come to believe about yourself in the core of your being. Your success or failure is undeniably linked to the words you say to yourself and the beliefs you hold about yourself. If you believe the truth, you will live with a self-concept that empowers and equips you to be effective. If you believe the lies of the enemy, you will be crippled in life by a limited and false self-concept.

So how do you begin to identify what you believe? Start by listening to what you say. Your mouth will reveal your mind! Jesus said, in Matthew 12:34, that "out of the abundance of the heart, the mouth speaks." If you will listen to yourself and really hear what you are saying about your- self, your life and your circumstances, you will be well on your way to knowing what you believe.

2. Become aware of how God wants you to think. You will become aware of how God wants you to think as you

> *Who you are in this world and who you will become boils down to the set of beliefs you have about yourself, and those beliefs—real or imagined—set up and define your self-concept, which greatly impacts your ability to fulfill your destiny.*

immerse yourself in the Word. From Genesis to Revelation, the Bible is full of cues and instructions concerning how we are to think. Remember Philippians 4:8, which I mentioned earlier in this chapter? Well, that's a good place to start. In that verse, God really specifies the types of things with which we are to fill our minds.

> *Keep repeating Bible verses aloud and silently, so that God's thoughts, as expressed in His Word, will become yours.*

Let's use two scriptural examples that reveal how God wants us to think. Look at 3 John 2, which says, "Beloved, I pray that you may prosper in all things and be in health, just as your soul prospers." Isn't that great? God wants us to prosper; we are to think thoughts of prosperity. Look also at Psalm 115:14, which says, "May the Lord give you increase more and more, you and your children." See, this verse helps you become aware that God wants you to think thoughts of increase. Keep looking at the Word to discover how God wants you to think.

3. *Focus your thoughts on God's thoughts.* Focus determines mastery, and in order to gain the focus needed to achieve your dream, you must align yourself with the Word of God. Broken focus can lead to failure and that is why the Bible admonishes us to be focused and single-minded, steadfast, immovable, unshakable, not wavering. Another word for focus is single-minded. We can learn the benefits of focus and single-mindedness by understanding what it means to be double-minded. James 1:8 tells us a double-minded person is unstable. That kind of person lacks focus, and is unsettled, undetermined, half-hearted, inconsistent, and wishy-washy. The distorted focus of double-mindedness will prevent us from achieving our dream—and that is not what God wants for us! He wants us single-minded and focused, keeping our thoughts firmly fixed on His. You will gain stability and the ability to achieve your destiny if you make the effort to keep your thoughts locked on to His.

4. Practice the thoughts of God until they are your own. In order to practice the thoughts of God, you will need to know the Word and meditate on it. Keep repeating Bible verses aloud and silently, so that God's thoughts, as expressed in His Word, will become yours. Because your actions reflect your state of mind, you will soon see yourself acting more and more like Jesus as you practice the thoughts of God.

5. Live the thoughts of God by incorporating them into the actions of your everyday life. If you are going to live your life according to the thoughts of God, you will have to not only know His Word, but also obey it. James 1:22 exhorts us to, "be doers of the word, and not hearers only," which means that we must act on the truth we read in the Bible. As you go about your everyday life, simply obey the Word in every situation. Living by the Word and expressing the thoughts of God in your everyday life is not as massive a challenge as it may seem. Just map your success and approach each step of your journey as a separate mission. As you do, keep obeying the Word and you will eventually arrive at your goal.

> *As you go about your everyday life, simply obey the Word in every situation.*

You're On

1. What are some of the beliefs you have about yourself?

_____
_____
_____
_____
_____
_____
_____
_____
_____

2. How does God want you to think?

_____
_____
_____
_____
_____
_____
_____
_____
_____

3. Are you focused on your dream, or are you double-minded? How will you improve in your ability to develop single-mindedness or increase the focus you already have?

_____

_____

_____

_____

_____

_____

_____

4. What practical steps do you need to take in your life in order to practice the thoughts of God?

_____

_____

_____

_____

_____

_____

_____

5. How can you incorporate the thoughts of God in one specific situation that is currently taking place in your life?

_____

_____

_____

_____

_____

_____

_____

_____

_____

Learn Your Lines

For My thoughts are not your thoughts,
nor are your ways My ways, says the Lord.
For as the heavens are higher than the earth,
so are My ways higher than your ways,
and My thoughts than your thoughts.
Isaiah 55:8, 9

For I know the thoughts that I think toward you,
says the Lord, thoughts of peace and not of evil,
to give you a future and a hope.
Jeremiah 29:11

Let this mind be in you which was also in Christ Jesus.
Philippians 2:5

But let him ask in faith, with no doubting,
for he who doubts is like a wave of the
sea driven and tossed by the wind.
For let not that man suppose that he
will receive anything from the Lord; he is a
double-minded man, unstable in all his ways.

James 1:6-8

COMING SOON

*S*ince your thoughts are so intricately connected to your destiny, how can you envision moving closer toward all that God has for you as you begin to align your thoughts with His Word? In what areas do you expect to gain victory? What kind of strength do you expect to see in yourself as you nourish dreams with God's thoughts and advance with confidence toward their fulfillment?

_____

_____

_____

_____

_____

_____

_____

_____

_____

_____

_____

_____

_____

ACTION!

*B*ased on what you have learned in this chapter, what are three concise, measurable, attainable goals you will set for yourself in the area of renewing your mind and getting your thoughts in alignment with God's Word? Be sure to include a schedule and target date for reaching each goal and a reward for accomplishing it.

1. Goal: _____

Schedule and target completion date: _____

Reward: _____

_____

2. Goal: _____

Schedule and target completion date: _____

Reward: _____

_____

3. Goal: _____

Schedule and target completion date: _____

Reward: _____

_____

8

The Lady Watches Her Mouth

Introducing

Do you know how powerful your words can be? They can "make or break" your dreams! Negative, depressing, hopeless words will lead to—well, negative, depressing, hopeless situations. On the other hand, positive, uplifting, encouraging words will lead to joy and peace and positive results. When you are on the path toward fulfilling your God-given destiny, you must speak words of life and success over yourself. As a leading lady, I also encourage you to speak words of life and success over other people—that is part of the way you lead.

In this chapter, I want to help you understand the power of what you say and to help you learn to speak success. As you fulfill the dreams God has placed in your heart, remember that by the power of your words, your tongue becomes a pen and can write your book of destiny.

The Main Event

Act 1: The Power of Life and Death

Your tongue is the tool that will bring you victory. Of course, it can bring you defeat, but I am believing that you are a leading lady who will use the power of the tongue to her advantage! Your words can build you up, or they can tear you down. They can propel you forward, or they can hold you back. You can use them to speak life and health and blessing to yourself and to others, or you can use them to speak destruction and discouragement. There's that much power in your words; you must choose how you will use them and whether your words will be a positive force or a negative force. They aren't neutral; they'll be one or the other.

Your words can build you up, or they can tear you down. They can propel you forward, or they can hold you back.

Proverbs 18:21 informs us that, "Death and life are the power of the tongue." Now that's a sobering thought! It tells us that, by our words, we can drown in our depression. Likewise, by our words, we can soar above the struggles and challenges of our everyday lives and ride the winds of blessings and praise. The tongue is a powerful object, and by our words, we form our destiny. In other words, what you say within yourself determines the end promise in your life.

You may wonder how something as small as the tongue can exert so much power in a person's life. That's because God has put the power of life and death in the words we speak. Read what the apostle James wrote about the power of the tongue.

Look also at ships: although they are so large and are driven by fierce winds, they are turned by a very small rudder wherever the pilot desires. Even so, the tongue is a little member and boasts great things. See how great a forest a little fire kindles! (James 3:4, 5)

See, just as the tiny rudder of a ship determines the course of the entire massive vessel, your words determine the course of your life. Just as a turn of the rudder can make a ship avoid dangerous waters, your words can also grant you safe passage through life if you will use them to speak life and blessing. But by the same token, just as a rudder would be capable to steering into an iceberg that would cause it to sink, your careless or foolish words could be your downfall as well.

Let me warn you that you are going to have to be disciplined and vigilant with your tongue. Every day is not going to be your best day. Along your journey toward destiny, you will encounter obstacles and attacks of the enemy. There will be times when you would really like to open your mouth and let loose with a whole stream of words that express your anger or your frustration or your impressions about someone or something. *Do not do it!* Do not allow your condition to take control of your words, but determine in your heart right now that your words are going to aid and abet your destiny; not hinder or destroy it.

Do you know how powerful your words can be? They can "make or break" your dreams!

You're On

1. Can you think of a situation in which your own words had the power of life or death on them—words that you spoke to yourself or to someone else?

_____

_____

_____

_____

_____

By our words, we can drown in our depression. Likewise, by our words, we can soar above the struggles and challenges of our everyday lives and ride the winds of blessings and praise.

2. Can you think of a situation in which someone else's words either gave life to you or brought death to a hope or dream inside of you?

_____

_____

_____

_____

_____

_____

3. What is the most life-giving statement you can think of to speak to yourself? Write it in the space below, then memorize it and speak it over to yourself often.

_____

_____

_____

_____

_____

_____

_____

_____

Do not allow your condition to take control of your words, but determine in your heart right now that your words are going to aid and abet your destiny; not hinder or destroy it.

Learn Your Lines

You are snared by the words of your mouth;
You are taken by the words of your mouth.
Proverbs 6:2

A wholesome tongue is a tree of life,
but perverseness in it breaks the spirit.
Proverbs 15:4

Death and Life are in the power of the tongue,
and those who love it will eat its fruit.
Proverbs 18:21

But no man can tame the tongue.
It is an unruly evil, full of deadly poison.
With it we bless our
God and Father, and with it we curse men,
who have been made in the
isimilitude of God. Out of the same mouth
proceed blessing and cursing. My brethren,
these things ought not to be so.
James 3:8-10

Act 2: Speaking Success

If you allow the words of the devil or negative people to penetrate your soul, you will lose your battle before it shows up on your doorstep. The enemy would want nothing better than for you to gripe all day. Do not fall into his trap and allow continuous negative words to cause you to miss your destiny. Attack back! Use your words as weapons to speak blessing, hope, and peace. God will back your words as you resist demonic assignments against you and against your dream. You have life in your words, so speak success!

Matthew 12:34 tells us that our words reflect what is in our hearts. If you have faith in your heart concerning God's plans for your life, you will notice yourself speaking faith-filled words. Silent faith is dead faith. For faith to operate, you must confess your faith out loud. Continue to declare what you have heard from the Lord that He wants to do in your life. Continue to declare what you believe, and it will build your faith. Begin to speak your life as a success, finding purpose and direction under the wings of God's protective hand.

God will back your words as you resist demonic assignments against you and against your dream. You have life in your words, so speak success!

I have practiced "talking out my destiny" for years and have seen its successful activity bring blessing into my life, my family, and my church. But it is possible to ask for things with the wrong motive or without holy living. If we live a life of compromise and pride, we will deceive ourselves into destruction. You cannot expect to get what you desire and speak if your heart is not right with God. For example, if there is unconfessed sin in your life, don't expect to see the good fruit of your positive confession until you repent. If you are resisting the Holy Spirit and being disobedience to His leading in a particular situation, you have no right to sit around spitting out mighty, eloquent faith-filled words and expecting a good result. Words are powerful, but they fall to the ground if you are not rightly related to the Lord and walking in obedience as you speak them.

As you've already learned in this chapter, you can do yourself great damage with the words of your mouth. So how do you protect yourself from bringing death by the power of your words or from hurting yourself with foolish talking? You speak success. I'd like to list for you eight habits to develop in your life that will help you speak success and exhibit an attitude of success through your actions.

1. Consecrate yourself daily to God.

2. Give God what is His, ten percent of your earnings.

3. Confess your sins if you miss the mark.

4. Ask God to fill your heart with His desires.

5. Avoid conversation with those who gossip.

6. Pray daily.

7. Read the Word.

8. Stay in an active church that feeds you.

> *Continue to declare what you have heard from the Lord that He wants to do in your life. Continue to declare what you believe, and it will build your faith.*

You're On

1. What specific areas of your life do you need to begin speaking success over right now?

_____

_____

_____

_____

2. Concerning your dreams and your destiny, what have you heard from the Lord and what do you believe? How can you speak success based on that revelation and on your convictions?

_____

_____

_____

_____

3. Is your heart right with God? If not, get it right today. Then begin to speak success!

_____

_____

_____

_____

Learn Your Lines

Pleasant words are like a honeycomb, sweetness to the soul and health to the bones.

Proverbs 16:24

For out of the abundance of the heart, the mouth speaks.

Matthew 12:34b

. . . God, who gives life to the dead and calls those things which do not exist as though they did.

Romans 4:17b

Let your speech always be with grace, seasoned with salt, that you may know how you ought to answer each one.

Colossians 4:6

. . . that the sharing of your faith may become effective by the acknowledgment of every good thing which is in you in Christ Jesus.

Philemon 6

As you fulfill
the dreams God
has placed in your heart,
remember that by the power
of your words, your tongue
becomes a pen and can
write your book of
destiny.

COMING SOON

I'd like for you to answer a very simple question as you think about what is coming soon in your life: How are you going to change your words in order to speak life to your dreams? Write down some of the words you will begin to say and how you expect them to impact your journey toward destiny.

ACTION!

*B*ased on what you have learned in this chapter, what are three concise, measurable, attainable goals you will set for when it comes to speaking life and success? Be sure to include a schedule and target date for reaching each goal and a reward for accomplishing it.

1. Goal: _____

Schedule and target completion date: _____

Reward: _____

_____

2. Goal: _____

Schedule and target completion date: _____

Reward: _____

_____

3. Goal: _____

Schedule and target completion date: _____

Reward: _____

_____

9

The Lady Wins Her Battles

Introducing

When you begin to change your mind and dare to dream, be prepared for all hell to break out against you. When God gives you a God-sized dream, He intends for you to be a threat to the kingdom of darkness. In fact, He intends for you to storm the gates of hell with passion and confidence and boldness as you fulfill His plans for your life. Part of being in God's family and being on the winning team in the age-old conflict between good and evil is that you will have to fight. Like it or not, the battle is raging; and if you don't know your enemy and know how to enforce his defeat, he will eat your lunch.

But know that your amount of success depends on your amount of adversity. The potential impact of your dream may predict the strength of your struggle. But no matter what kind of opposition comes against you, you know that you will win. Remember that Jesus came to destroy the works of the enemy (1 John 3:8b) and remember the promise of 2 Corinthians 2:14, which says that God *always leads us in triumph* in Christ" (italics mine).

The Main Event

Act 1: Know Your Enemy

The devil has come to steal, kill, and destroy your destiny. That's right. John 10:10 tell us that the enemy (the thief) "does not come except to steal, and to kill, and to destroy." As I shared with you in Chapter 1 of this workbook, the enemy is not out to get you as a person; he is out to steal your dream, to kill your potential, and to destroy all the God-given possibilities that exist within you.

The *Spirit-Filled Life Bible* offers a word study on Satan, and teaches us that Satan is "An opponent, or the Opponent; the hater; the accuser; adversary, enemy; one who resists, obstructs, and hinders whatever is good. Satan comes from the verb which means 'to be an opponent' or 'to withstand.'" (*Spirit-Filled Life Bible*, ©1991, Thomas Nelson, Inc., p. 710). He is a deceiver, and as the Bible also calls him in John 8:44, "a liar and the father of it," which means he is the father of lies.

> *When you begin to change your mind and dare to dream, be prepared for all hell to break out against you.*

He will scheme to find your source of strength and resource. He will try to prevent you from reaching your destiny in God, but he will not succeed. On your way to triumph, though, you will no doubt face many obstacles—and that's a good sign; it means you are being an effective warrior in God's kingdom and for His cause! Even though he is a liar, a deceiver, a murderer, a thief, and a fierce opponent of your dreams, He is also defeated! Jesus has already defeated him. You have been destined for greatness, and the devil cannot stop the plans of God from coming to pass. God will hide you in the cleft of the rock. He will protect you in every attack, and He will show you a way of escape! You will not die prematurely and God's dream for your life will not be aborted.

I need to tell you that you are not likely to ever encounter the devil as a little red man with horns on his head and a pitchfork in his hand. No, he is far more subtle than that. Maybe he will come to you disguised as a great business oppor- tunity—but one that will drain you financially. Maybe he will come to you as an irresistibly handsome man, who is either determined to wreck your marriage or draw you into an unhealthy relationship. Maybe he will speak lies to you through your friends or family, who constantly tell you that are not good enough, smart enough, or something- else enough to accomplish the dream in your heart. You must know the truth of God's Word so well that you recognize the lies of the enemy, no matter where they come from. You must be so intimate with the voice of God that you know instantly when the enemy is speaking, regardless of how smooth he talks. And you'll have to resist him and be determined to keep right on dreaming. Below are some examples of what you might have to say to him as you wage war over your destiny:

> *Satan is "An opponent, or the Opponent; the hater; the accuser; adversary, enemy; one who resists, obstructs, and hinders whatever is good. Satan comes from the verb which means 'to be an opponent' or 'to withstand.'"*

> *I need to tell you that you are not likely to ever encounter the devil as a little red man with horns on his head and a pitchfork in his hand. No, he is far more subtle than that.*

♦ "Devil, you can cause somebody to handcuff me, I'll still dream!"

♦ "Devil, you can cause somebody to walk out on me, I'll still dream!"

♦ "Devil, you can cause somebody to break my heart, I'll still dream!"

♦ "Devil, you can cause somebody to lie to me, I'll still dream!"

♦ "Devil, you can cause somebody to talk about me, I'll still dream!"

♦ "Devil, you can cause somebody to degrade me, I'll still dream!"

♦ "Devil, you can cause somebody to take my money, I'll still dream!"

You're On

1. According to John 10:10, what are three things the enemy comes against you to do?

_____

_____

_____

_____

_____

2. What are some of the meanings of the word Satan?

_____

_____

_____

_____

_____

_____

_____

3. What is the enemy really after: you or your dream?

_____

_____

_____

_____

_____

_____

_____

_____

_____

Learn Your Lines

For though we walk in the flesh,
we do not war according to the flesh.
2 Corinthians 10:3

For we do not wrestle against flesh and blood,
but against principalities, against powers,
against the rulers of the darkness of this age,
against spiritual hosts of wickedness
in the heavenly places.
Ephesians 6:12

For this purpose the Son of God was manifested,
that He might destroy the works of the devil.
1 John 3:8b

Act 2: Strategies for Victory

I really want you to fulfill your destiny in God and to see your dreams come true, so I want to share with you some strategies for victory as you fight the good fight and obliterate the obstacles that try to hinder you. Let me give you three simple steps to receiving strength to fight and win the battle for your dreams:

◆ Admit you cannot do it alone and that you need God's help.

◆ Confess that there is nothing too hard for God.

◆ See yourself doing what God has asked you to do.

Admit you cannot do it alone and that you need God's help. Confess that there is nothing too hard for God. See yourself doing what God has asked you to do.

In addition, there is no substitute for prayer, worship, and much time in the Word as you are in the midst of spiritual warfare. Even as you are fighting, commune with God; and spend a few moments praying, praising, or simply enjoying the presence of the Victor. Stay firmly grounded in the Word, and find scriptures that will empower and encourage you for the specific situation you are be experiencing.

I also want to share with you three more strategies for victory. These are also mighty weapons against the enemy!

1. Learn from Your Opposition

Look at what happened to Joseph when he told his jealous brothers about one of his dreams. Genesis 37:8 says: " . . . So they hated him even more for his dreams and for his words." Let me tell you something: Hate is very informative. I'm serious! If you can discover what your enemies hate about you, you can pinpoint what makes you so valuable. Do not allow your enemies to see more of your value than you do, but find out why they hate you and let them help you realize why you are so dangerous to the enemy's camp.

2. Keep Moving

If you are going to hold on to your dream, the fulfillment of God's plan for your life, then you are going to have to keep moving. Whatever you do, don't stop. The enemy's strategy is to bring you so much pain that you are paralyzed.

That's why you must always keep moving toward what God has for you. Let the dream propel you and allow the voice of God to call you out of yesterday's struggles into your destiny. Keep choosing to move in the direction of your dreams. No matter how difficult it may be, just get up and take a step forward. If the best you can do is take a shower, take a shower. If the best you can do is write ideas on paper, write them. If the best you can do is go to Bible study, go. Even when you don't feel like it, trust God enough—and believe in your dream enough—to do *something* to move toward it.

Learn from your opposition. Keep moving. Live in the Yes Zone.

3. Live in the "Yes Zone"

When I tell you to live in the Yes Zone, I mean for you to learn to respond to God by saying "Yes!" to Him all the time because you have such a deep knowledge and conviction that He is totally in control. Respond to Him with a "Yes!" when doors are open and with a "Yes!" when doors are closed. This is the epitome of trust in God, and it allows you to survive painful moments and accept things you do not understand. Romans 8:28 teaches us that, ". . . all things work together for good to those who love God, to those who are called according to His purpose." You love God, and you are called according to His purpose. Therefore, you can be assured that all things are working together for your good. That should give you the confidence to say "Yes!" to everything God allows and orchestrates in your life.

You're On

1. Are you using the mighty weapons of prayer, worship, and the Word? If not, I encourage you to start now. They will make a difference!

_____

_____

_____

_____

2. What have you learned about yourself from those who oppose you and seek to hinder your destiny? ("Those" may refer to the devil or to people).

_____

_____

_____

_____

3. What are you doing to keep moving along the path of your destiny? If you are "stuck," ask the Lord to show you how to get back in motion.

_____

_____

_____

_____

_____

_____

_____

_____

4. Are you living in the Yes Zone? If not, when will you start?

_____

_____

_____

_____

_____

_____

_____

_____

Learn Your Lines

For the weapons of our warfare are not carnal,
but mighty in God for pulling down strongholds,
casting down arguments and every high thing
that exalts itself against the knowledge of God,
bringing every thought into
captivity to the obedience of Christ.
2 Corinthians 10:4, 5

Therefore take up the whole armor of God,
that you may be able to withstand in the evil day,
and having done all, to stand.
Stand therefore, having girded your waist with truth,
having put on the breastplate of righteousness,
and having shod your feet
with the preparation of the gospel of peace;
above all, taking the shield of faith
with which you will be able to
quench the fiery darts of the wicked one.
And take the helmet of salvation,
and the sword of the Spirit, which is the word of God;
Ephesians 6:13-17

No one engaged in warfare entangles himself
with the affairs of this life,
that he may please him who enlisted him as a soldier.
2 Timothy 2:4

COMING SOON

I want to ask you to use the space below to respond to this Bible verse: " . . . forgetting those things which are behind and reaching forward to those things which are ahead, I press toward the goal for the prize of the upward call of God in Christ Jesus" (Phil. 3:13, 14). What will it mean for you to "press on"? How will you push back when the enemy presses against you and your dream? How sweet will your victories over him be?

_____

_____

_____

_____

_____

_____

_____

_____

_____

_____

_____

ACTION!

*B*ased on what you have learned in this chapter, what are three concise, measurable, attainable goals you will set for yourself as you fight and win your spiritual battles and contend for your dream? Be sure to include a schedule and target date for reaching each goal and a reward for accomplishing it.

1. Goal: _____

Schedule and target completion date: _____

Reward: _____

_____

2. Goal: _____

Schedule and target completion date: _____

Reward: _____

_____

3. Goal: _____

Schedule and target completion date: _____

Reward: _____

_____

10

The Lady Guards the Dream

Introducing

As long as you live and march toward your destiny in God, you will have spiritual battles to fight. Now that you have learned, in Chapter 9, a little bit about who your enemy is and how to gain victory over him, I'd like to focus in this chapter on how to guard your dream. You are the only one who can protect the dream inside of you, and you know by now that the enemy is more determined to kill and steal your destiny than he is to afflict you as a person. Over the next few pages, I'd like to help you build a fortress around your dream so that nothing and no one can stop it from coming true.

The Main Event

Act 1: Beware: Dream Killers!

You have a responsibility to protect your dream, and one effective method to safeguard your dream is to know and recognize the enemies of your dream. Second Corinthians 2:11 suggests that Satan can get an advantage over us if we are not aware of his tactics and devices. We need to know what some of the tools are that he uses to try to dismantle a person's destiny.

Did you know that everything under the sun has natural enemies? There are parasites that survive by preying on other organisms. They victimize, plunder and destroy others for their own gain. Some are so small that they cannot be seen with the naked eye, and seem so insignificant that a person could easily ignore or disregard them.

The same may be true of people or situations that would want to kill your dream. Germs and viruses are with us all the time! A person may seem harmless and docile, but actually be full of venom and determined to keep your dream from coming to pass. Be discerning about people and be careful about the situations you get into. Remain prayerful so that you can spoil the plans of the enemy.

In order to guard your dream and discern these enemy agents, you will need to use the "microscope" of the Spirit. If you try to figure everything out in your mind and do not discern in the Spirit, you could become overly sensitive and cautious and then end up paralyzed by fear. The enemy will use any weapon against you—even you. So make sure that you are using spiritual discernment and not soulish paranoia as you examine the people surrounding you and your dream.

> *You have a responsibility to protect your dream, and one effective method to safeguard your dream is to know and recognize the enemies of your dream.*

As I'm sure you realize, your most effective offensive weapon is to walk in the Spirit. Stay clean before the Lord, keep your mind renewed by the Word, apply godly wisdom to your circumstances, pray as often and as fervently as you possibly can, worship in every situation, and avoid striving in the flesh, but trust God to bring His good purposes to pass in your life.

Even though this workbook has already addressed the importance of renewing your mind, I want to remind you that the thoughts you entertain in your mind can—and probably will—affect your destiny. Many times, we damage our dreams unintentionally because we fail to guard our eyes and ears. I need to tell you that the things you see and hear can choke your dream. Do not let low language, filthy speech, or negative talking pass through your "ear gate." Do not let perverted scenes, displays of violence or dark, depressing images pass through your "eye gate." Slam those gates and give no place to the devil. Keep your hearts and minds pure. Be cautious what you watch on television or in the theater. If you are struggling with areas of sin, it makes no sense to let the media fill your mind with those thoughts. They can be dream killers, so lock your doors against them and keep them out!

> *Stay clean before the Lord, keep your mind renewed by the Word, apply godly wisdom to your circumstances, pray as often and as fervently as you possibly can, worship in every situation, and avoid striving in the flesh, but trust God to bring His good purposes to pass in your life.*

> *You must remain determined at all costs to guard your heart and allow your dream to develop in the incubator of your spirit.*

I will say to you again that the enemy wants the dream inside of you. Your challenge is to guard your heart, as Proverbs 4:23 says, because your thoughts, your actions—and therefore your dream—spring from it. You must remain determined at all costs to guard your heart and allow your dream to develop in the incubator of your spirit. When you do, be assured that Satan will send assassins after your dream. But you can learn to use his attack to your advantage. It can make you stronger and help prepare you to fulfill your destiny. Recognize your dream killers, stay on guard; walk in the Spirit—and watch God turn to good what the enemy meant to harm you.

You're On

1. What specific dream killers are operating in your life right now?

2. What can you do to protect your dream against them?

_____

_____

_____

_____

_____

_____

_____

_____

3. Are you guarding your eyes and ears? If not, what are you letting in? Do you need to stop watching certain television shows, stop reading steamy romance novels, or stop letting the ungodly principles in rock, rap, pop, R and B or country music into your heart through your ears?

_____

_____

_____

_____

_____

_____

_____

Learn Your Lines

Keep sound wisdom and discretion;
so they will be life to your soul
and grace to your neck.
Then you will walk safely in your way,
and your foot will not stumble.
When you lie down you will not be afraid;
yes, you will lie down
and your sleep will be sweet.
Proverbs 3:21b-24

Keep your heart with all diligence,
for out of it spring the issues of life.
Proverbs 4:23

. . . lest Satan should take advantage of us;
for we are not ignorant of his devices.
2 Corinthians 2:11

Act 2: Share Selectively

One of the most exciting things in life is to discover your destiny, to know the dream God has put in your heart. But let me warn you that your dream may not be nearly as exciting to the people around you as it is to you. Do you remember what happened when Joseph shared his dream with his brothers? ". . . they hated him even more for his dreams and for his words" (Gen. 37:8). His brothers were so jealous that they wanted to kill him after he told them his dream!

Most of the time, those who do not support you and your dream will fail to do so because of their own woundedness. They may be jealous; they may be intimidated; or they may be afraid that your pursuit of your dream will change the relationship they currently enjoy with you. They may think you cannot do anything right or that you are disqualified because of your age, your race, a physical handicap, or a past failure. You cannot let someone else's struggles affect you or your destiny. Have mercy on the wounded and pray for them, but do not let them stop you!

Think about Peter when he climbed out of the boat to walk on the water. He exhibited much more faith than anybody who stayed in the boat and watched. He may not have made it all the way, but he made it farther than all the rest. He exercised some faith, but the others exercised no faith. When you get out of the boat, you put the people inside the

> *One of the most exciting things in life is to discover your destiny, to know the dream God has put in your heart. But let me warn you that your dream may not be nearly as exciting to the people around you as it is to you.*

boat in an awkward position. They must now justify why they are still in the boat. Don't listen to them! A quest for the acceptance of people can be disastrous. Often people will suppress you or hold you back to justify their own weaknesses.

Your dream is your most valuable possession. It belongs to you and no one else. No one can take your dream away from you *unless you delegate that authority to them.* People, however, can certainly affect your self-confidence, and consequently your desire, to fulfill your dream. So remember, be careful who you share it with! Don't allow anyone to minimize your dream, and don't trust your dream with just anyone. If they can't rejoice over it, don't share it with them. If they can't encourage, promote, or help cultivate your dream, keep it to yourself. When you do share it, choose wisely those people to whom you will entrust your treasure. Make sure they are healed and whole enough to not be jealous or intimidated. Be certain that they can and will support you and cheer you on as you walk in and enjoy the fullness of what God has for you.

Now is probably a good time to examine the people you share your life with and the people who influence you. Do they draw you closer to God or pull you away? Your relationships will often determine your choices. Your choices will determine your destiny. Ask God to show you who you should be connected to and who you should not be.

For example, think about Samson. He did not lose his strength overnight. He did not say one day, "I don't need God anymore. I can do this thing by myself." No, it was a

> *A quest for the acceptance of people can be disastrous. Often people will suppress you or hold you back to justify their own weaknesses.*

steady, daily routine of just ever so slightly giving in to the enemy through his relationship with Delilah. A spirit of compromise is slow and subtle. It wears at you daily until you let your guard down, and then the enemy attacks.

Are you in a relationship or particular situation that could cause you to compromise or to miss your destiny? Too many times Christians put themselves into situations in relationships because of the need for companionship. At some point you must work through your barriers and build healthy relationships. Let your life be filled with God and He will satisfy your needs for strategic relational alliances and for companionship. He also knows exactly who to connect you with to help advance His plans and purposes for you.

> *If they can't rejoice over your dream, don't share it with them. If they can't encourage, promote, or help cultivate it, keep it to yourself.*

You're On

1. Even though you will only want to share your dream with certain people, you do need to be able to articulate it clearly—even if you only say it to yourself. In one or two sentences below, write down what your dream is.

_____

_____

_____

_____

2. As you think about guarding your dream and using wisdom as you share it with others, who do you think you should not share it with right now?

_____

_____

_____

_____

_____

No one can take your dream away from you unless you delegate that authority to them.

3. Who are the cheerleaders in your life, the ones with whom you can share your dream, knowing they will wholeheartedly support you?

_____

_____

_____

_____

_____

_____

_____

_____

Learn Your Lines

Wise people store up knowledge,
but the mouth of the foolish
is near destruction.
Proverbs 10:14

Do not speak in the hearing of a fool,
for he will despise the wisdom of your words.
Proverbs 23:9

O Timothy! Guard what was committed
to your trust, avoiding the profane
and idle babblings
and contradictions of what is
falsely called knowledge—
by professing it some have strayed
concerning the faith.
Grace be with you. Amen.
1 Timothy 6:20, 21

Every good gift and every perfect gift
is from above, and comes down from
the Father of lights,
with whom there is no variation
or shadow of turning.
James 1:17

COMING SOON

*S*omething good happens when a woman begins to take responsibility for her own dream. As she guards it and protects it, it becomes more precious to her, and its fulfillment becomes even more important. As you think about guarding your dream, what kind of strength do you think that will produce in you? What are you going to start doing to protect that which God has put in you?

ACTION!

*B*ased on what you have learned in this chapter, what are three concise, measurable, attainable goals you will set for yourself as you guard your dream? Be sure to include a schedule and target date for reaching each goal and a reward for accomplishing it.

1. Goal: _____

Schedule and target completion date: _____

Reward: _____

_____

2. Goal: _____

Schedule and target completion date: _____

Reward: _____

_____

3. Goal: _____

Schedule and target completion date: _____

Reward: _____

_____

11

The Lady
Keeps the Faith

Introducing

God has dealt every person alive a measure of
faith—and that includes you. God gives it to us
so we can develop it and become productive in
our every day walk with Christ. He gives it to us so
that we can hold on to the dreams inside of us and pursue them
with passion and diligence. If you are going to fulfill God's
great purposes for your life, you are going to have to have faith.
You know by now that your dream will not go unopposed, and
faith is going to be necessary to contend for your destiny.

The Main Event

Act 1: Never Give Up

Faith is the substance or the guarantee that those things
which you are waiting for will come to pass. Faith is the evi-
dence when we cannot see the manifestation. Faith begins
when you drown your doubts, cast off your fears and anchor
yourself in truth. So many people make the mistake of depend-

ing upon their senses for making their decisions, but it is your faith that determines your decisions. And your decisions will determine your destiny.

God is faithful. He is not like the people you meet every day who talk big, but have short memories. If God has promised you something, it will come to pass. There may be a waiting period, but it will come to pass! I believe that many people throw in the towel and quit just before they break through to the promise God has for them. It is through faith and patience that you inherit the promises. So hold on—your blessing is on the way!

As you develop faith, God will declare something to you as a point of revelation. Then, as you look at your situation, you realize that what He has declared has not yet happened.

Faith begins when you drown your doubts, cast off your fears and anchor yourself in truth.

You wait a while and look again—and it still has not happened. This can cause you to doubt, to become frustrated, to become impatient, and even second-guess the revelation. But your current situation cannot predict the fulfillment of the revelation; you just have to have faith and continue believing that it will come to pass. What God says will happen is going to take place. Don't give up if you are waiting—that's what it means to have faith.

No matter what comes your way, you can make it become a pathway to destiny. Choose to face your current battle and determine in faith to make it a bridge to bigger and better things. Whatever you do, never give up. Keep doing all you know to do, and remember that you might be disappointed if you fail, but you are doomed if you never try. The enemy may try to abort your destiny prematurely, but what God has destined for you the devil cannot stop. Do not submit to fear and believe his lies. If God has promised you something, remember that God cannot lie. You will get there; keep the faith. As the saying goes, "I have read the back of the book, and we win!" When that becomes truth to your understanding, you realize that your pursuit of your dream is not in vain. Press on, leading lady friend. Do not give up, for in due season, God shall reward you for your labor of love.

It takes more faith to walk through a struggle than to be delivered from it. I may not be able to stop things from happening, but I can do something about my attitude toward them. It really does not matter what you go through; what matters is how you go through it. You see, storms do not break us—they make us. The process of faith is the ability to endure. But remember, faith is by grace, not something you obtain or produce through works. It is not something you must work to conjure up in your life. No, your faith is dependent upon your trust factor, and your trust factor is determined by your relationship with Christ. Fill your life with faith by getting to know God.

> *If God has promised you something, it will come to pass. There may be a waiting period, but it will come to pass!*

You're On

1. How strong is your faith?

_____

_____

_____

_____

Choose
to face your
current battle
and determine in
faith to make it a
bridge to bigger
and better
things.

2. Has your faith been worn away or weakened by attacks of the past? How can it be rebuilt?

_____

_____

_____

_____

3. What is it that God has so clearly called you to do that has made you determined to never give up?

_____

_____

_____

_____

Learn Your Lines

Therefore, my beloved brethren, be steadfast,
immovable, always abounding
in the work of the Lord,
knowing that your labor is not in vain
in the Lord.

1 Corinthians 15:58

Now thanks be to God who always leads us
in triumph in Christ,
and through us diffuses the fragrance of
His knowledge in every place.

2 Corinthians 2:14

And let us not grow weary while doing good,
for in due season we shall reap if we do not lose heart.

Galatians 6:9

Fight the good fight of faith, lay hold on eternal life,
to which you were also called
and have confessed the good confession
in the presence of many witnesses.

1 Timothy 6:12

*You see,
storms do
not break
us — they
make us.*

171

Act 2: How to Persevere

I can hear you now, saying, "Pastor Paula, I know I can't ever give up, but it gets so hard sometimes. *How* do I persevere?" I'm glad you asked; I want to share with you several ways you can exercise your faith and persevere until the promise comes.

> *Just because God has called and created you to do or be something does not mean you won't have to practice and develop your skills in that area.*

1. Be persistent. Don't expect to "win" the first time you try something or every time—even when you know you are destined to succeed at it. You've heard the old saying, "Practice makes perfect," and just because God has called and created you to do or be something does not mean you won't have to practice and develop your skills in that area.

2. Stay in the Word. Study the Word to learn who God is, how He moves, and what He does. Keep studying the Word and meditating on its truth as a part of your commitment to never give up.

3. Keep seeking God with your whole heart. Pray. Lean on Him. Let the Holy Spirit guide you as you learn how to listen to His voice. Once you get an understanding of His Word, then you begin to declare the Word aloud.

4. Remember that, as you speak the Word, you hear the Word and it activates faith. The Word feeds your faith and starves your doubts. You build yourself up each day and then do it again the next—and just keep doing it. Faith says, "I can make it. I trust Him. I will do it."

5. Remember that God is faithful to fulfill all His promises. Though they linger, tarry. Wait on the Lord, for His promises are sure. He sent His Son, our Savior, as He promised; and He sent His Spirit, as He promised. He will fulfill all that He has promised you.

6. Recognize that it is not your spirit that is full of doubt and unbelief—it is your mind, your will, and emotions. Your spirit will believe. Your spirit believes whatever God says. Your spirit man can take your mind's limits off of God. Your spirit will always believe God. Your spirit is inundated with grace; and grace brings, as a gift, faith.

Keep studying the Word and meditating on its truth as a part of your commitment to never give up.

7. You may need to do something for someone or give something away. You may be believing for a new house, a new car, a new job, and have been praying for years. But "faith without works is dead" (James 2:20b). Pray and ask God what it is that you can do or give. Part of your perseverance may be an act of faith that involves giving. Hosea 4:6 says, "My people are destroyed for lack of knowledge." So many Christians are uninformed about God's instructions. Once you know and understand the spiritual laws of sowing and reaping put in motion by a sovereign God, you cannot stay bound by poverty and failure.

If so, I want to encourage you to start living the life of a faith-filled believer. All the promises of God are yea and amen to them that believe. 2 Corinthians 9:6-8 in the Amplified Version says, "Remember this: He who sows sparingly and grudgingly will also reap sparingly and grudgingly; and he who sows generously, and that blessings may come to someone, will also reap generously and with many blessings.

If you are struggling, let me kindly, but forwardly ask you, "Are you giving to God what is His?" Friend, God doesn't need your money. You need God's money. The system for blessing is giving. Start giving your best today.

8. Trust God to carry you. He is the Guide, and when we cannot go on any longer, He carries us to our destination. You can always count on the strength of His wings, for they will never let you down. The term "eagles' wings" is symbolic of God's strong and loving care in Scripture (Is. 40:31). The eagle watches over its young in the most careful manner, flying under them when it leads them from the nest, lest they should fall on the rocks and be injured or destroyed. The mother will fly under the young to act as a guide on the journey. If the young should become weak or weary, the providing mother will carry its young back to the nest upon her back. That's the way God is with us.

Finally, remember that your faith will be tested and you will need to persevere. But the product of the testing of our faith, the faith we have after we have been tried or tested, is considered here to be more valuable than gold. 1 Peter 1:6 states, "In this you greatly rejoice, though now for a little while, if need be, you have been grieved by various trials . . . ."

Remember, this faith walk is a process, and God is using every trial that comes your way to refine you as a priceless possession more precious than gold.

These "trials" will come so that the impurities of your carnal nature, which hinder your faith, may be refined, removed by the fiery process. When you are going through a trial, it seems like it will never end. After you have reached the other side and can look back in hindsight, it was only for a little while.

"Be of good cheer," Jesus told us. In fact, those were the words He spoke to His disciples not long before He went to the Cross. He was facing the most tremendous trial any human being has ever encountered and had just informed His disciples that their lives were going to change radically. He said to them what He says to you today: "In this world you will have tribulation, but be of good cheer; I have overcome the world" (John 16:33). Remember, this faith walk is a process, and God is using every trial that comes your way to refine you as a priceless possession more precious than gold.

Wait on the Lord, for His promises are sure.

You're On

1. Are you practicing the skills you need in order to live your dream with excellence and skill?

_____

_____

_____

_____

_____

_____

_____

2. Chances are, there is some area in your life in which you are having to wait on the Lord. How are you doing with that? How can you wait more patiently or more proactively?

_____

_____

_____

_____

_____

_____

3. Is there anything God is asking you to do or to give right now? When will you do that?

_____

_____

_____

_____

_____

_____

_____

Learn Your Lines

For we walk by faith, not by sight.
2 Corinthians 5:7

*Therefore we also, since we are surrounded
by so great a cloud of witnesses,
let us lay aside every weight and
the sin which so easily ensnares us,
and let us run with
endurance the race that is set before us.*
Hebrews 12:1

. . . but I press on, that I may lay hold
of that for which Christ Jesus has also laid hold of me. . . .
one thing I do, forgetting those things which
are behind and reaching forward
to those things which are ahead,
I press toward the goal for the prize
of the upward call of God in Christ Jesus.
Philippians 3:12-14

But you must continue in the things
which you have learned and been assured of,
knowing from whom you have learned them,
and that from childhood you have known the Holy Scriptures,
which are able to make you wise for salvation
through faith which is in Christ Jesus.
2 Timothy 3:14, 15

In this you greatly rejoice, though now for a
little while, if need be, you have been grieved by various trials,
that the genuineness of your faith,
being much more precious than gold that perishes,
though it is tested by fire, may be found to praise,
honor, and glory at the revelation of Jesus Christ.
1 Peter 1:6, 7

Your dream
will not go unopposed,
and faith is going to
be necessary to contend
for your destiny.

Coming Soon

What is that you have faith for in your life right now? What do you need faith for? Would you use the space below to write about what you are believing God to do in your life?

_____

_____

_____

_____

_____

_____

_____

_____

_____

_____

_____

_____

_____

_____

_____

_____

ACTION!

*B*ased on what you have learned in this chapter, what are three concise, measurable, attainable goals you will set for yourself as you grow in faith? Be sure to include a schedule and target date for reaching each goal and a reward for accomplishing it.

1. Goal: _____

Schedule and target completion date: _____

Reward: _____

_____

2. Goal: _____

Schedule and target completion date: _____

Reward: _____

_____

3. Goal: _____

Schedule and target completion date: _____

Reward: _____

_____

12

The Lady Births the Dream

Introducing

When you are anticipating your birthing, opposition may arise. The enemy will attempt to abort your pregnancy with destiny. But there is an appointed time, a set time, or a due season. Don't settle short of what God has for you. It's a new season; it's a new day!

Once you have given birth to destiny, provision will follow. Your gifting will be recognized. Your calling will be discerned and confirmed by others. Others will be raised up to protect your vision while it is being developed. You can trust His plan, for all of heaven's resources are backing you.

Isaiah said that God knows the "end from the beginning," (46:10). That means that before you got started, God knew your ending. He knows exactly what you need to bring to birth and He will give you the strategy and the energy to do it. It won't be long now!

The Main Event

Act 1: It's Not Just Your Baby

You are pregnant with a dream. Maybe you've been pregnant for a long, long time. Your dream started in the womb of your spirit, and, at the proper time, the birthing process must begin. Jesus is the Alpha and the Omega, right (Rev. 1:8)? That means that whatever He started in you, *He will finish.* I believe that your moment of greatness has come, and that the blessing of God is upon you to prosper and succeed.

> **Jesus is the Alpha and the Omega, right? That means that whatever He started in you, He will finish.**

God never required anyone to do a miracle, only to begin one. Too often we look at what we have as insignificant and cannot see how it can help anyone. God is not lacking in resources. He enjoys sharing with His children, and His nature is to increase. He just needs a vessel to work through. Your destiny is not just for you, you see, it is for a far larger audience and a far greater reason. The dream that you are birthing is for the purpose of blessing others and, most of all, for bringing glory and honor to Jesus Christ.

You are like Abraham—you are blessed so that you can be a blessing to others. I encourage you to live the life God's called you to and to bless everyone and everything you come in contact with. Possess your promise so that both you and others can benefit from it. You just don't know who may be waiting on you, watching for you, or counting on you. You don't know who else's dreams depend on yours.

You know by now that your destiny won't just drop in your lap. You will have to birth it, and just as happens when a woman gives birth in the natural, you will have to push in order to finally hold your dream—the dream that will bless you more than you ever imagined and extend beyond you to bless others. When the time comes for your dream to become reality:

◆ Push aside the shame!

◆ Push aside the small thinking!

◆ Push aside the boundaries!

◆ Push aside the rejection!

◆ Push aside the discouragement!

◆ Push aside the lack!

◆ Push aside the past!

◆ Push aside the hardship!

◆ Push aside the lies!

◆ Push aside the depression!

> *Your destiny is not just for you, you see, it is for a far larger audience and a far greater reason.*

You can do it in the name that is above every name, the mighty name of Jesus!

Believe God today for His anointing to flow through you and to push through everything that would hold you back from walking in His purposes, blessing others, and giving Him glory. Receive a spirit of boldness, strength, and might. Receive the spirit of the warrior for Christ, the spirit of the Captain of the Hosts, Lord Jesus Christ. Receive the spirit of victory, so that you can walk in everything God's dreaming for you.

You're On

1. What is it that the Lord has started in your life and that you are believing Him to finish?

_____

_____

_____

_____

_____

_____

_____

Receive the spirit of the warrior for Christ, the spirit of the Captain of the Hosts, Lord Jesus Christ. Receive the spirit of victory, so that you can walk in everything God's dreaming for you.

2. What is the purpose of your destiny, aside from being a blessing to you?

_____

_____

_____

_____

_____

_____

3. What do you need to push aside right now in order to birth your dreams?

_____

_____

_____

_____

_____

_____

_____

_____

Learn Your Lines

For a dream comes through much activity, . . .

Ecclesiastes 5:3

*. . . God, who gives life to the dead and calls those
things which do not exist as though they did.*

Romans 4:17

*being confident of this very thing, that
He who has begun a good work in you
will complete it until the day of Jesus Christ.*

Philippians 1:6

Act 2: Worship All the Way Through

As grand as your destiny is and as wonderful as walking in it will be, I need to tell you that God calls you to an even higher place than that. He calls you to the secret place, a place where intimacy can be developed and true worship nurtured. And your ability to worship is crucial as you birth your dreams and as you enjoy their fulfillment. No matter what others do or say, do not lose the passion for His presence. No matter what happens as you give birth to your dreams, keep going to the brook—the streams flowing with living waters. Slow down and take a deep breath. Let God quench the thirsting of your soul and keep you refreshed. No one can satisfy you or encourage you like Jesus.

You push with your praise.

Birthing is a grueling, intense process and along the way, you will have to push through some obstacles. You push with your praise. In those moments, you are offering a "sacrifice of praise." Let me tell you, though, simply singing a song to the Lord doesn't always classify as a "sacrifice" of praise because it is easier to sing a song when all the bills are paid, there is money in the bank, and none of your loved ones are in the hospital. But what song do you sing when things aren't going well? Do you pull out a "blues" tune and walk around saying "woe is me?" That song isn't a sacrifice of praise.

The sacrifice of praise looks at those things that stand in the way of your destiny and then looks to a God who is bigger than all that. The sacrifice of praise reflects not your feelings or your situation, but your God. The sacrifice of praise might even include some dancing, shouting, and lifting up your hands. This type of praise can quickly set you free. Throughout the Bible, praise has been a source of victory (Josh. 6; 2 Chron. 20). There is power in praising

God. Praising the name of Jesus sends fear into the enemy's camp. Giving God glory and honor lifts up your spirit. Giving the Lord your highest praise causes angels to move to fulfill God's Word and help bring His purposes to pass in your life.

But it is important that we understand what giving praise to God really is. Praise is not a fast song, and worship is not a slow song. Praise is thanksgiving and worship is intimacy. The power to praise is realized when you realize that despite your circumstances, you choose to be thankful. So incite a riot of praise! Your thanksgiving will create a relationship of trust, and trust is easy when you know the character of God. So start thanking God for your opportunity, your new shoes, your new dress, your new car, your new home, your new job, or your new ministry. Bless His Name!

> *The sacrifice of praise looks at those things that stand in the way of your destiny and then looks to a God who is bigger than all that.*

Your worship, as I've just written, is different than your praise. Worship is your gateway to the throne room of God. Worship is an act of your spirit going into the presence of God. When a believer meets with the Father, the experience is unforgettable. In His presence, you don't ask for what you can get from Him. You don't ask for anything. You simply enjoy His company, simply spending time with Him personally and intimately.

In worship, you are meeting with God in a private place. Worship does not require a physical location where you can go in seclusion to have a special prayer time, but rather a secret place you can go in your heart to meet with the Most High. Out of these secret meetings—out of the privacy of

> Out
> of these secret
> meetings—out of the
> privacy of your
> worship—comes the power
> and the strategy to birth
> your dreams and live
> them as the world
> watches.

your worship—comes the power and the strategy to birth your dreams and live them as the world watches.

In the place of worship, the Lord will do all kinds of things for you, without your even realizing it. He will often heal you of your woundedness; He will let His goodness wash over you and bring you wholeness; and He will move you closer and closer to the fulfillment of your destiny. You're not asking for it; it just happens. When your spirit is open to His Spirit, you will certainly change for the better and you will advance in the direction of your dreams.

You're On

1. How is your current love relationship with God? Are you enjoying His presence in intimate worship? If not, what can you do to put yourself in a position to do so?

_____

_____

_____

_____

_____

_____

2. As you birth your dreams, what areas of your life need the "push" of praise right now?

_____

_____

_____

_____

3. According to what you have just read, what is the difference between praise and worship?

When your spirit is open to His Spirit, you will certainly change for the better and you will advance in the direction of your dreams.

_____

_____

_____

_____

4. Would you take some time to stop right now and simply praise and worship the Lord?

_____

_____

_____

_____

_____

Learn Your Lines

Oh, worship the Lord in the beauty of holiness!
Psalm 96:9a

*I will extol You, my God, O King; and I will bless
Your name forever and ever.
Every day I bless You,
and I will praise Your name forever and ever.*
Psalm 145:1, 2

*"Not by might nor by power, but by My Spirit,"
says the Lord of hosts.*
Zechariah 4:6

*Now to Him who is able to do exceedingly
abundantly above all that we ask or think,
according to the power that works in us,
to Him be glory in the church by Christ Jesus
to all generations, forever and ever. Amen.*
Ephesians 3:20, 21

Rejoice in the Lord always. Again I will say, rejoice!
Philippians 4:4

Don't settle
short of what God
has for you. It's a
new season; it's a
new day!

COMING SOON

*W*ell, here we are. You've made it all the way through this workbook, and I am believing that you are ready to birth your dreams. Indeed, quantum leaps toward the fulfillment of God's plans and purposes for you are coming soon. Related to your destiny, what do you long for and expect to see in your life in the days to come?